FAME

SAINT JULIAN PRESS

POETRY

Books by KEVIN MCGRATH

Fame (1995)
Lioness (1998)
The Sanskrit Hero (2004)
Flyer (2005)
Comedia (2008)
Stri (2009)
Jaya (2011)
Supernature (2012)
Eroica, and *Heroic Krsna (2013)*
In the Kacch, and *Windward (2015)*
Arjuna Pandava, and *Eros (2016)*
Raja Yudhisthira (2017)
Bhisma Devavrata (2018)
Vyasa Redux (2019)
Song Of The Republic (2020)
On Friendship, and *Causality In Homeric Song*
(forthcoming, 2023)

F A M E

KEVIN MCGRATH

SAINT JULIAN PRESS
HOUSTON

Published by
SAINT JULIAN PRESS, Inc.
2053 Cortlandt, Suite 200
Houston, Texas 77008

www.saintjulianpress.com

ISBN-13: 978-1-955194-12-9
Library of Congress Control Number:

Cover image: Ioannis Hamaris, 1963,
courtesy of the Benaki Museum Athens.
Author Photo: Courtesy of Akos Szilvasi.

FOREWORD

FAME in this book does not concern a quality received or acquired but an understanding of how the *kosmos* functions, an active mental awareness of how it is that the universe occurs in terms of metaphor. For if there is only one narrative in this world—one book and all works of art attempt to emulate or imitate that pattern—then it is the work of poetry to pursue that ideal sonority, integrity, and radiance. No one comes as close to an appreciation of *fame* as the youthful Achilles with his unspeakable grief. The ancient world—in the Hellenic or Indic model—was one that was preliterate, premonetary, presecular, and so unlike how it is that we deliberate action and experience emotion today. Then, the natural and supernatural were not distinguished, not in terms of terrain or climatic conditions, for there were no such distinctions. That is the world of FAME, that apprehension of a uniform material agency which inspired the poets with both visual and acoustic discernment. This book originated in the pedestrian landscapes of New England, on the coasts of France and in the Eastern Mediterranean, in the terrain of Western India, and in the old Caribbean archipelago: for topography is always the source of our most primary metaphor. There are many seas and oceans in this poetry and the experience of many long marine passages. Ultimately it is the beauty of a man and woman who share not simply their happiness but their mutual observation of what they are not, that joins us all equally. It is their strange and unique apperception which is so impulsively unique and momentarily complete. That bound consciousness is a moment of volition in which a human being becomes aware not only of his or her acute autonomy but of a certain terrestrial recognition, causing us to be vigilant, alert, apart from ourselves and so perpetual.

FAME

I – 1

A BIRD flew to the air
The great chamber was empty
All the shadows had fled
And all the hours were in shadow

Shadows you were
Dressed clearly like grain
Grain and thirst
The bird of conceivable space

I - 2

THERE are four winds about the world
That move within the human soul
First - the strange attraction going
Between a girl and boy

The second takes us on in time
So that we might look back
At the residence and procession
Of what is lost upon our way

The third is the emptiness that
Fills up our breathing days
As we go toward our source
Its quietness makes us more still

The final air is that of beauty
Quick ephemeral always true
The breeze that makes substantial
Everything we do not know
Song of what we cannot say

I - 3

I LOVE that beauty shall be beautiful
And admire your lovely truth
Ambivalence and ambiguity which
Compose the margins of a human soul

The vivid elements and mastery
Of life imbued and balanced
Where observation finds its pleasure
In the slow tact of your motion

Obedient to darkness you
Possess all genius of goodness
You are the love that finds itself
Coherent with beauty's movement
Gracious as light itself
As it fills the world with vision

I - 4

THE intrinsic stain of human life
Is more than a golden thread
All boys and girls know this
Loveless dust of the world
As they reach to hold a hand
Or catch an eye's submission

The unbearable human soul
Clothed in a palpable body
Craving another's touch
An oblivion of smooth warmth
And fluid of its softest tissue
Bird of exquisite plumage

You once yielded all desire
And promises perpetual
Day is long and life is short
Yet the pleasure of the soul
Demands constant renewal -
Do we possess sufficient joy

All the children of the earth
Can smile and shake a finger
Young women might glance
As the young men stare
But when the dust is blown
And the clothes removed
And the bird of love vanishes
What can the lifeless soul declare
What promises are heard then

I - 5

So much water goes past
Flowing downstream slowly
Rain snow flood all
Make for a river's rising

Yet when we come to a bank
Go out in our narrow boat
And bending down to taste
How little we catch to drink

So much current flowing
Through earth's ancient arteries
Turning to salt experience
On reaching the great ocean

How little touches our lips
Running out from fingers
Yet born with a thirst we are
Always going toward water

I – 6

DOES beauty exist in water
Can it be seen in the sky
Or is it passing through the air
As light breaks into spring
When the wind is most on fire

Beauty goes with timeless measure
With feet unseen to living eyes
One slight human defect
Causes its transit to be undone
Upon a burning axle of days

Is there beauty in a child's
Perfection of uncovered limbs
Or in glances shot between
Young men and women's eyes
When shadow is a lucid blue

Beauty shows herself to those
Who do not expect to stay
Beyond the effort and the anguish
That make for life without end
On a dancing floor of this place

A sweet delicious comb of light
Of soft white generative tissue
In whose weightless substance
Is beauty to be briefly found
In ways that we cannot say

Beauty exists in movement
In every transient thing
In beauty there is slowness
Brevity lightness and
One great absence of desire

This is a truth transparent
Equality of how time solves
Separates and divides us from
All that is coherent here
Where beauty finds itself
Strangely wandering the world

I - 7

IF beauty is all slowness
Our life vanishes in haste
If we might only pause
Earthly loveliness would be
More apparent and its truth
Take on formal weight

In stillness lies our cause
The forceful decency of life
Hastening we lose ourselves
And the particles of time

On the one hand is decay
And on the other is duration
Love is our infallible guide
As vision reveals balance -
How the human spirit weeps
Soul dripping from our eyes
As it witnesses the racing

I - 8

FOR a short time an endless moment
Two swans swimming down a river
Or as two gold lions pace
The shore-line of an empty coast

So too in time these present days
When the tissue of spring is torn
A world puts on its fiction and
Its lovely tinted new illusions

Crimson leopards walk at night
Beneath heavy dripping trees
As optimism - like a bird
Or certitude - flies from the moon

May we always keep this rest
As a constant inner world
Where marriages are only true
Renewed each day with satisfaction
And the warm river never ends

I - 9

Of all extant beauty
Dark star without possession
Whose lovely cruelty retreats
Covering itself inside light
We are poured out the river
Tells me - at this lilac time

As you - my bride in the air
Whose currency exceeds
Sweet black cavities of night
You and I pretend
Thinking we are discrete

We are a music others hear
Being carried on elsewhere
Finding ourselves unmoving
Abundantly concealed by
These great white hours
And all their complex going

I – 1 0

IF the soul has no shadow
And our light on earth
Is only moving and transparent
Making us rise up from
False nameless dark
Suddenly aware and desiring

As a wind blows careless
Through immaculate distance
In a tall hyacinth sky
Shaking gold flowers
On a yellow May morning
Affecting how we observe

Innocent and barely new
Gently exposed in my arms
Beautiful and most assured
One being of the future and
Two rivers in a life flowing
From ancestral suns and days

Quick with light you are
Weightless and so feminine
Daughter of beauty and goodness
Restoring our good breath
With one just heart-beat
And your optimism

My delicate sparrow
I am caught in a mesh
Surprised by complete love
Informed by your promise
Of all possible kindness
Unshaded by guilt or remorse

Young and perfectible
Veiled bride that you are
Offering us true life
Accept in your sleep
My grateful ambition
Here - as I take your hand

I – 11

YOUR gentle sleeping innocence
Whose mild breath inaudible
Whilst dawn sprinkles rain
Upon lately risen light

Frugal fallible a new world
Before it is to be described
Defenceless ingenuity of
Unsimulated artless calm

Undisclosed without coercion
Your freedom that is unaware
Where youth and sleep are entire
Context for earth and life -

No one in the world has seen
You so at rest and undisguised
And as time does not recur
This instant is without record

Tenderness is a sign perhaps
Of creativity itself
Imperfect not repeated
As a future amplifies a past

Where your womanhood remains
Inhabiting and uncovered
More of friendship than desire
Yet completely satisfied
Recipient of all balance

I – 1 2

As we lay upon a shore
Naked in the smooth hot light
A blood-warm ocean rolled
Recursively on coral sand

Stained with phosphoros and kisses
Nuptial powder on our skin
You made the darkness tuneful
My lioness of silk and tissue

In the coppery rites of sunset
You were my soul and universe
In those instants we became
Infinite and changeless

Before dawn raised its eyes
Exposing so much truth
From senseless prolific night
As the sun's panels slid apart

Among the columns of the sea
Its restless frantic tongues
We were quietly recognised
And our transparency noted

Time removes all experience
But for a slightest trace
The strange delays of life and
Its lamps and intervals

Within a few simple moments
There is treasure folded deep
And the rest of life is sequence
There are no errors in love
In the ultra and aquamarine

I – 1 3

THE sowing of men and women
Spontaneous irresistible
Now in this month of fall
As trees reveal a spectrum
Colours of lost desire

As with a field and furrow
Where grain is scattered by hand
We bury the future in darkness
Entering into night

This knitting together of tissue
Flesh and earth and time
With you I turn inwards
We close the doors retire
Our promises on fire

I – 1 4

EARTH would show her cities
If asked to reveal herself
Monuments embankments
Bridges and all the statues

A river upon which life
Has flooded and receded
A brown vein distended
Wealth trade and flotsam

Nothing is more fair than
Timeliness of being
Passion and corruption
Art refining each desire

A red dawn swells above
Becomes a pure opacity
Cold air is fine and damp
Vigorous with old life

Swept away in this flame
Earth relights her loving
Beauty that is dark and bold
A stone spire of humanity

The river's mud is bitter
Spawning this essential
As millennia of ambitions
Run by with their lust

for Harriet Bridgeman

1 – 1 5

ONTO the zero lake they came
Down from a low nacreous sky
Their gentle faces soaked with space
With lucid skin and transparent bodies

Not a living soul was in sight
As they sang of pity for humankind
Grey drops that fell from their eyes
Were like soft young herons in flight

As we hurried off along the shore
Seeking minutes somewhere else
They observed our necessary guilt
And wept for our foolish haste

In suspense above an emerald lake
Engrained hovering they wait for us
For we are their myth and without them
We are untrue without consequence

They admire our easy friendship
Feeding us their light wafers
As their spirit like two snakes
Twines throughout the universe

Their weightlessness sustains us
The duration of humanity
Till one day they repossess
Our strange causeless ways

I – 16

SOON the swans return and
Shall descend upon the lake
Gracious slow circling down
Towards these cold grey waves

Signs of life they are
Touching upon a spring
With an archery of insight
That strikes recumbent winter

With so much languid treasure
Gathered by long flight
These inhabitants of sheer air
Know of life's migration

They do not give but offer
To those who see their way
Who silently beside the lake
For years await this presence

Great white birds who wheel
Gliding down without sound
As one by one they circle us
Made speechless by their beauty

Far from a distance they
Bring warmth and consciousness
So human spirit can abound
In light and kindness and
Being that in time is just

I – 17

I HAVE seen things in my life
Which no one else has known
How to say this now - how
To speak of what is vision
For so much is unheard

I have looked across a river
And seen them there - those
Who have no human name
Whose language has no word
Faultless with compassion

As birds of unblemished wing
Perfect with unearthly tone
They shoot across the candid air
Their shining bodies lucent
Propelled by light and shadow
Their unfinished songs
Are speechless full of love
Floating far above our haste

Beautiful they are and gracious
Luminous within their skin
As if no worldly life could be
Possessive of such warm body
A supernatural being walks
Inside their easy going

Their clear sureness is
Vibrant in a flawless manner
Generous gentle undemanding
Nothing can inhibit them

In their experience domination
Never can secure a place
So constantly - we must admire
Observing time in how they play

I – 1 8

As a shell that lies upon a lake
Broken into dust and time
Or mist that dissipates in heat
When white sun warms the ground

So rain falls upon a river
As a slow current runs away
And human life evaporates
Leaving but a few drops

How passion and affection go
Disappear so lightly
As if there was no love
And no mystery occurred

Just like an empty shell
Where coldness and cynicism
Lie curled up in a little space
The moral beauty of the world
Is dissolved by slight darkness

I – 1 9

THE small terrors that enclose each day
Genius of time avoiding us
The art by which we struggle onward
To triumph through such emptiness
Love with which we build a house

These are the stones that we arrange
Signs of loneliness and solitude
When despair removes all sensual life
Enveloped by deep silence
We review the void of living

Time is ruthless - how it wounds
Our words are broken by the days
We polish all this desolation
To make a flimsy world accept
A powdery shore and vital place -
There is no love but only vision

I - 2 0

THE entirety of human love
Outlaw impatient artless
A seam in which we freely
Choose to run our hand
Joining with the durable

This is the end the moment
Origin and conclusiveness
The surface of duality as
Our only way to correspond
Our bitterness at fragility and
How the formless crouches
Far within the heart of form

1 – 21

THEY come and go and trespass
Freighted with desire
Young women of the spring
In their summer dresses

Crocus yellow hyacinth
Their golden shoulders bare
A green text burning
Sweet upon their lips

A mysterious and complex grace
The pleasure of your smile
The girl in you pretending
That you are not alone

Be with me beside you now
With the future's breath
In our sleep we shall resist
And admire the fugitive
We shall complete the world

I – 2 2

THE nature of my love is this
I witness you as no other
When you are mine to hold
Refining our warm volume

I love your bones and your smell
A scent of leaves and rain
At the hollows of your joints
My hands confess their love

Asleep with you I have no
Other place on earth to visit
You are all world and home
Ground where life sets out

What more is there in time
For us to know - what else
Can human love accomplish
In you I touch an absolute

I brush your lips with my tongue
Breathe in your exhaled breath
Deep inside we perceive
What no one else observes

I – 2 3

LAST night as you lay beside me
The most beautiful of women
I felt that I was at home
On earth – mortal and empowered

My concord and my platinum
My peerless assertion
You - my perfect boundary
My liaison with all of time

A spray of rain upon the dark
Bloodless obdurate sky
Outside our room was nowhere
Space lay warm in my arms

Your legs alongside mine
Our ankles touching casually
My hand upon your smooth back
As you fell asleep and sighed

Is there justice in our love
Genius or honesty in life
Last night I was transfigured
By your immense equilibrium
As I looked upon your smile

I – 2 4

LAST night I held in my arms
The most beautiful thing on earth
Night of a full May moon
When life once more ascends

Not joy nor love nor possession
Nor the giving up of passion
Nor the first lie that made this
Neither regretful nor worldly

Touched by warm living beauty
Whose curve bent over and rested
Beside me the sleeping breath
Moved on my lips and face

Beyond any pattern of minutes
Beyond that invisible wall
When as a heap of dust we are
Dispersed by a friend or lover

Last night beauty and goodness
Faultless fruitless generous
Gave itself to my guilty heart
As a window opened on space

One indestructible night
Further than human expression
Gentle stable desiring to be
Held before it was lost

I – 2 5

To sleep with you in my arms
Intimate warm and tender
Your breath upon my mouth
Your hair upon my shoulder

Sweetness of your topaz skin
Closeness of your perfect bones
How you move in the night
As all a world inaudible

Milky light of low morning
Its citron rays piercing leaves
Silence of day as animals
Retire to sleep or hide from us

We who have so very much
Wealth from an original aeon
Our gold has no currency
But the gestures we exchange

I - 2 6

Do you remember the pink oleander
And the hot breeze of an afternoon
A courtyard's breathless shade and
Jasmine darkening a night with sweet

Do you remember the cool of vines
Beneath which we sat and watched
As bamboo switched in the air and
A turquoise sea crackled and flashed

How cicadas screeched and rasped
During noon's white ferocity
Moonlight made a world abstract
Monochrome with silver candour

Do you recall the lemon blossom
In the square as we walked home
From the port at night - you and I
On that island without a name

I put some oleander by your bed
Before you woke one morning
Furtively I watched you sleeping
Flirting beside a watering stream
In your mind you were not with me

Where are the paths and groves now
And the heated dust on our skin
And afternoon behind walls when
We lay down in a shuttered room
Wakening to bathe at a cistern

I – 2 7

THE faint blur that we leave
Upon time and space
Fragrance of rain at night
A sudden meteor falling

You wakening slowly
In your bare white room
Breaking your illusions
Motionless in sleep

From far off I watch you
A bird climbing the sky
Premonitory quiet waiting
For you to notice me

Like light I shall enter
Into your day your heart
You will not know that
I have settled inside

Suddenly you will need me
And I shall be there - but
It all happened long ago
And we are just the trace

I – 2 8

WE shall meet in paradise
You and I when all this is done
And the rains have gone and
The wet roads and low dawns
And winter has crystallised
Become a blue midsummer
An aerial flashing ocean

Until then let us keep
Nights companionable and
Let us walk together down
More paths than we know
Keeping close and private
Each furthering the other

For we shall see in paradise
All the time on earth
And we shall be like trees
Golden knowing everything
Our senses like white birds
Possessing what is unstable
Here in a shifting world
The circles will be ours and
Each thread of our bodies firm

I – 29

WHAT marvel is there more than you
Your golden armour and your guilt
The gentle snarl provoking love
When I see you in the arms of one
Who has you more complete than I

But he could never hold you as
In my heart I phrase you now
In my hands I rule the tongue
Which makes you more than life

I imitate and I repeat
And marvellous I make you more
More than beauty - more than pleasure
More than warmth that's his to hold
Central him but mine to touch with every thought

I - 3 0

My heart is a three-masted boat
A virgin of green and blue seas
With five sails bent and drawing
And foam splashing from her stem

You are my ship and voyager
Image of lights charting heaven
In my heart you were fearless
Then another took you away

Islands that smell of perfume
Trees that shine in dark hours
Houses built of sharp white coral
These I thought would be home

He has you now tied by a thread
And seas are unbearably calm
My heart sails alone and bitterly
Dignified - avoiding harbour

You are still my passage bird
Wheel I hold in my hands
The soul may dissolve into salt
But the ship is made to go

1 – 3 1

WHAT is the incidence of love
When the three stars fly out
When deception becomes the rule
That is not to be avoided

Bare trees filter golden dawns
Fretting still molten light
You are alone without illusion
What can you say to equivocate

Fugitive yet pointless - turning
About to see a perspective
Forgetting becomes a creative act
In order to meet with success

Without the impetus of love
You are a ghost - stalking one
Everything you mutter aloud
Holds two separated meanings

What is the instance of love
And those stars where are they
Into what sphere do they go
When you hold out your arms

I – 3 2

THOSE who seek perfection in love
And in this are always failing
Dispossessed unsatisfied blackened
By what it is they imagine

Is it the experience of beauty
Something tangible beyond life
Or is their vision amoral unearthly
Leading to this vast displeasure

Perfectly attuned and tranquil
Caught in silence and dimension
Discontented by bodies which
Do not calm their immense desire

Two horses lashed to a wheel
Chasing circulating darkness
Escaping only drives them onward
To repeat the same patrol

I – 3 3

ANXIOUS primitive and undesiring
Days fall like yellow leaves
Under the rain onto the roads
They rush away into oblivion

How is it that we recall them
And triumph over time's vacuity
A recollection that reforms us
Makes us alive again heroic

Language with its nets and hooks
Pictures with their strange shadow
Slowly we recapture the creatures
Who ran away one stormy night

Wandering out there in wild nature
Troubled by their strange solitude
We entice the days back toward us
To sleep again under one roof

1 – 3 4

IN paradise there are no mirrors
For none need to reflect
Nor are there any memories
Life and days are complete
And nothing is forgotten

Love has a secret to perfect
Intimate and undisclosed
The private ring a suitor gives
To one distinguished bride
Genius informing him
With ideas to accomplish

I have no place on earth - he says
No kind recollection only
A strange affiliation for
All that I see before me

I give myself to you having
No other living wealth
You are my joyous vision
My rest and every resolution

Your beaches and your coasts
Islands and fringing hills
Your pink dawn and setting suns
Air light wind birds these
I marry to my distance
For space is all I comprehend
Endless sleepless compulsion

I - 3 5

AERIAL flowers of evening fall
Indigo powder of night comes
Uniform formless and attractive
Compelling and suggestive

The stiff blue silk of August
Imprinted with courting birds
Has become limp and colourless
The sky lightless with space

Summer with its azure eyes
Its green shadows and pools
Its mercury light filled us
Most happily with illusion

If we polish the soul daily
A world can be reflected
Both intimate and abstract
Being constantly bewildered

Night with all its brightness
Shining and so perfumed
It satisfies our longing for
That most refined of images
The invisible heart's clear bell

I – 3 6

WE are like water you and I
Running through the gorge of time
Unconsumed between white rocks
And smooth bones and black snakes
Where only eagles look down
Running out toward the sea

If in many years to come
You return and wander here
I shall be with you in kind
Beneath the arching sunlight
For you are always in my heart
And I am now like these stones

As you descend the deep path
In the hot silence of noon
I shall be watching hidden
Like the lions on the hills
For time and beauty were fulfilled
Within our affection

For there are just two cities
Where a gorge runs between
I have gone ahead and wait
Where a clear sun never sets
Where we shall always walk
Among the olive groves through
Long fields towards the ocean

I - 3 7

CICADAS pigeons and sound of bells
Suddenly the dawns of long ago
Return fresh and uncluttered
As if today were simply renewed
And no one had ever gone

No one had vanished and love
Not lost its promised shape
No one descended into darkness
Never to walk on earth again
Or look the sun in the eyes and smile

Life passes but for the plea of children
Voices of women the prolix sea
Cicadas telling of just one story
Of how much we possess except
For the consciousness of so much beauty

I – 3 8

My daughter for all her loveliness
In her light-filled weightless way
Laughs and listens to a music
That no one else perceives

Her destiny is beyond me yet
She rests in my arms as we
Walk the grounds at night beneath
An ingenuous saffron moon

Small grains of genius and love
Enter her gentle sanctuary
Unseen they pause and settle there
Till one day they put out leaves

This is the secrecy of time
How immortality finds a place
How it is that truth adheres
Becomes transmitted between souls

Unaware of the freight we bear
Its indifference and monotony
Our reckless life and impatience
Reveal an easy timelessness

We do not know what we convey
Of universal privacy
Forms of beauty and of music
Like the unison of love itself
Are prescient with sunlight

I – 3 9

SHE appears in the world as if
From an envelope of the same
And as a girl she is composed
By small gestures of affection

In youth she learns to imitate
Before she learns to pretend
Dazzled by masculinity she
Offers herself as its place

Only once in her life is a woman
Given by hand in marriage
And then she lightly appears
Supernatural in her beauty

As a wife loving provides her
With a vision of potential
How it is to move in time
Without being distracted

Then with her children she
Assumes more than she knows
Giving more than she possesses
She is mutual with the world

She grows pliable as her family
Acquire their own desires
A matron she revives pleasure
Acting without converse

At last as a widow she is
Generous easy with laughter
For betrayal and ordeal have
Exposed the nature of virtue
And the power of her words

I - 4 0

As the sun enters the lion
Chromium dust filters evening
Time becomes like a dim water
Where we go without saying
Upon a glittering reflective sea

The nerveless unconscious ocean
Where life thinks of nothing
Disembodied and pleasurable
Lust is simply visible
And there is no efficacy

Where the soul leaves a body
Mourning the memory it deserts
Naked without desire as
It hurtles through night and space
Towards unimaginable islands -

Where the sun never settles
And there are only white birds -
Lion of human luminosity
Going lightly among the hours
Beneath the eyelids of long day

1 – 4 1

A REARING lion like a magnet
Draws the soul into itself
Years gather slowly round
Touch their forehead to the earth

Once there was a life that tried
To clarify the names and words
In its vision of a world
To triumph with a simple point

Brazen light of morning sweeps
The globe like a dancing place
A flat bright disc upon which
Creatures meet to kiss and part

Leopards rise up and sing now
Panthers at night are monotone
Eagles bend their necks down
Both in praise and mourning

Love will take us on and straight
From struggle or what we destroy
Love that never shudders when
Dissolved by a voice in the fire

Hope was a hull made of leaves
Belief the bubble in its compass
Transmitted it told its story
Suspended between waves

The lions disappear at once
Their image hovering on the air
Invisible beauty gathers close
Waiting for the next call
When humanity cries out

for Philip Sherrard

I – 4 2

To emulate the cry of love
Its carnal wish inborn to life
What is it we should say
That knows of no reply

With daring or with cynicism
Which blows through space
Moving being - act effect
Or condition - every call

So many cattle of the soul
Driven from a potter's wheel
Onto a sea of burning white
Raise their heads to speak

What will free us undo silence
Catching us upon its round
Is there a love that will loosen
Pleasure that will go beyond

My god - the terror of this place
Is there nothing we can say
Extinguished like a match
We are not to be repeated

I – 4 3

WHEN every passion vanishes
Adhesive to the human heart
No longer prey a soul
Is dustless and undying

The hawk of spirit rising
Like fire it enters light
An impulse purely heat
As the food of time

Fearless and intangible
Folded throughout space
The soul assumes the traveller
Who meeting any creature
Equals the desire to play

I – 4 4

WHERE is the boat I do not see it
The banded moon is already there
Did you weep stepping aboard
Was the passage complicated

Are there lemon trees growing
And white birds among the bells
Do you feel refreshed and strong
Having shed your old worn skin

The orange blossom must smell sweet
Erotic thanatic the leaves pungent
How is it when there is always light
Sunless sleepless without change

Perhaps they were the oars I heard
Slow locks squeaking and dripping
As I woke before dawn yesterday
And your house was all closed up

for Gordon Miln

I – 4 5

THE saffron fragrance of the ocean
The effulgence of its space
The undyed depths whose origins
Like memory are not to be discerned
Where all lives remain unknown

The red sails of antiquity
Aeons of quiet suffering
And our joy when the sea
Procreates endlessly for us
Milky waves forever breaking

The sea seduces us with
A pitiless complete beauty
Without demands without gifts
Without content and unconstrained
Offering to us its own image
A perfume that exceeds all
We might ever know on earth

I – 4 6

BOATS are coming out of the light
Into the roar of human suffering
Yet here and there points of love
Shine and sparkle lucidly

There are no surprises any more
Nothing to redeem our ways
A plenitude of struggle and hope
Leaves us alone on a vacant shore

It is not that time passes us by
But we who recede from time
Constant and immutable it
Leaves us only glancing

Then it is not love we see
But strange ghosts who are made
In our image as we grow quiet
No one knows why we do as we must

There is so much beauty on earth
Transporting us out of our lives
Yet when the boats come to take
Our thin bare souls away
Beauty is silent and only withdraws

I – 4 7

BOOMING down towards Kythera
With five sails bent and hauling
A white hull through the waves
Breaking ultra and aquamarine

With you beside me at the wheel
And all of life behind us
The island on our starboard bow
Within a coruscating distance

The apex of our known world
Quivering on the horizon
Amorous together – you and I
Among the groves and saplings

Our anchor firm within a bay
Riding out the warm nights
A ruined citadel upon the cliffs
Outlined by constellation

What is the extent of time
With which we are provided
As I hold you in my arms
The vessel rocking in the dark

How to make the voyage last
Beyond anything we know
What words are possible now
That can take us further

Beyond Kythera towards where
Our boat will sail herself
Out of time's circumspection
Fluctuating in the light
Where our fame will always go

I – 4 8

HOURS on the ship timbers creaking
As the boat swayed and lunged
Into a damp marine night running
The vessel remorseless unthinking
Engines beating like blood
Sails rattling and cracking as
The mast-head dipped like a stylus
Among pure white inky stars

Hours on the ship with you
Down in our wooden cabin
Falling asleep beside you
Our bodies wet with love
In a saffron dawn that streamed
Through a small porthole
You moved closer against me as
I inhaled your sweet warm breath

Hours on the ship as if
There was no land nor earth
We became strangely infinite
The flying-fish and the flags
The bells and circling weather
As night after night below
Folded into our quiet selves
We rose and fell oblivious
Intimate with an ancient ocean

I – 4 9

As the soul flutters away from its ashes
Insensible helpless powerless
Purified of this doubtful life
By being washed with cleansing fire
Is there any single thread attaching
Us to a lightless ungraven being
Or are we translated repeatedly

Old shipmate companion voyager
Where are we bound on this ocean
As the boat sinks away from sight
Into a grey-green and bluish deep
And the last smoke rises from shore
Towards what new life are we destined
Naked without women or shadow

The heroes have wandered far away
Gone in search of those whom only
They were able to call and love
An unburnt dust of remaining friends
Hovers about a rough damp pit
Keen and thirsty to drink of blood
Released from the cycle of truth

We are free of bodies for just a while
Before we suffer these worlds again
Perpetually changing upon a coast
Between sea life and desiring death
Necessity was the wheel of our passion
As soul arises to frequent the air
To annul our further migration

Nature draws us with implication
Strips us and leaves us under the sun
On a pebbled beach where like lovers
We enjoy the heat of a shimmering day
As cicadas rave inland on rocks
And lust bleaches our souls dry
Discharging the ancient guilt

All things come at last to a chasm
Where carnal justice cannot exist
Solemn unclothed affection of youth
Bare immemorial pathways
All forgetfully ruined
As we leave behind the universe
Entering a pure black void of nil

Old mariner pilot captain of time
Seven seas and a white vessel await
Shake out the canvas and throw off
Those anchors and useless oars
Let us embrace the horizon and go
Beyond the ultimate fire of zenith
Where none will recognise our spirit
And soul like a quick white bird is gone

for Richard Warren Vick

I - 5 O

UNDER the olive trees of old youth
We loved and slept and transformed
As along the coasts and on
Stony sunlit hills we wandered

The necessity of imperfection
In all our breathing life
In the slow struggles we engage
In order to arrive somewhere

We forget and abandon days
When hours were limitless
In a continuous fading of beauty
Becoming continual darkness

There is blackness to be endured
If we are to reach eminence
An oblivion of human emptiness
Until that vivid light returns

Suddenly those dancing trees
Appear and surround our steps
And upon that earth and shadow
We once more rest a while
As time leaves us alone again

I – 5 1

ALL those who in life have gone
To the shore of the sea of being
An ocean of potential where
They forever patrol the coast
Awaiting further commands

A molten sky and shadowless ground
Turbulence of invisible waves
A grey-blue unoriginal light
Where life takes its primary pulse
The quiet roar of everything

All the nights in one's life do not
Always end with the dawn
Sometimes we find ourselves
On the margins of an absolute sea
Where a sun can neither rise
Nor set and only souls dwell

I – 5 2

HOW all of experience only
Deceives us with its air
Glistening impermanence
Duplicity of two worlds

We live as in a gateway
Like a watchman sleeping
As past and future travel
In and out of a city

Into our open mouths
So much water is pouring
Never to be consumed
Nor to allay our thirst

How wonderful is time
Gorgeous like a kingfisher
Quick brilliant and gone
Before we glance twice

In solitude we struggle
With giants and armies
Shadows we perceive
Consider to be true

If the sun has a memory
Let it now awaken us
You and I pretending
We are going nowhere
And the city absolute

I – 5 3

LIKE giants bowed in anxious thought
My memories of you sit about me now
Weighing my shoulders and oppressing
All attempt to recall your presence

Sometimes they cry and move around
And in my sleep you return to me
Wakening there remains no trace
Just the same grey motionless figures

If we are a glass which holds the dust
Measuring out our time on earth
Sometimes the giants turn us and
We can reclaim some of our laughter

So many grains of memory
Crowding into a single room
Ponderous unquiet in their oblivion
Unconscious solitary shapes who
Are unaware of you and me

I – 5 4

THE immortals are all about us
Yet they do not know their names
Sometimes it is their suffering
Their loneliness and remorse
That releases them from being
The desperation of this place

Then they perform their worth
Their music and their words
With vision and compassion - love
Pacifying and conceiving for
We who live and walk the earth
Remain obscured by flames

Their genius and lightness go
Sovereign and easily
The quietness and softness of
Their joy is for us so firm
Beautiful and kindly as
They reflect their force upon us

Inscrutable and undestined
Enduring darkness in the world
Their despair for an earthly void
Illuminates our hesitation
With signs of slowest passion
Then one day they are gone and
We recall them in human prayer

I – 5 5

NOT just a single beauty
But all the passing states
The various and manifest
Each day another form

Once in flamingo
Another time a heron
Soaring through the quick light
Or as a sparrow laughing

Her beauty was ephemeral
Never once paused
So many women were
In her body as she walked

Blue as a kingfisher
Who shot out her glances
With so much rapid grace
Then each day she vanished

When I held her in my arms
She changed before my eyes
Lucid and transforming as
She was not here on earth

How I loved this woman
Who was always receding
Drawing me away from
The time that I knew well

One morning I awoke
As she lay beside me
And then at last I saw
Her beauty deep inside
As all the world approached

I – 5 6

IN a soft blue cyanine light
As I walked out one afternoon
Herds were passing beneath trees
The land hovered in dust and heat

I walked for miles the powdery ways
A few hawks swooped to see me
And then returned across the earth
Between thorn and dry hedges

Upstairs in a cool dark room
Shutters locked against the sun
You were resting with eyes closed
And candidly I lay beside you

Finding perfection in your arms
Your slowness like rain
As you lightly rest asleep
With my hands I adore you

I walked among the trees at night
Singing of my admiration
As beneath the perfect sky
You and I strolled at dusk

The threads of our desiring
Tangle and knot themselves
I am fixed by your beauty
Your simple easy form

As owls in the fruit trees
And peacocks in the deep grass
Warily observe your calm
And listen to my words telling

So I am bound and tied up
By loving you and keeping
Beside you as we cross these fields
Yet there is no real going

For how is it I cannot
See myself and yet perceive you
And in my eyes at night
Your beauty is my world

Shadows gather in the leaves
As we pass through the orchard
Small snakes avoid our footfall
As silence gathers round

Wind moving in the foliage
Like rainfall sounds on pebbles
My voice your breath the air
All these mix and this is pleasure

Sleep – and I shall always sing
As I look upon your features
You are more than I have known
All affection and surrender

As light reaches nadir or
A bird vanishing in space
So my passion counters you
As it introspects your days

Like a reflex concealed
Or the fruit of being human
As you rest in my arms untroubled
I shall be your instrument
As we cross the enduring earth

I - 5 7

As we sat upon a hill-top
Amazing at its vision
Flat land for miles receded
Between ocean and plateau

So much time lay beneath us
Sheathed in lucid space
Years and their endeavour
Their doubt and anxiety

Now we were justly balanced
As beneath us flocks and herds
Quietly roamed the terrain
With no place on earth

Prophecy and its glare
Fell away from those hours
Above the distant glassy lakes
And that gentle frugal ground

A hare bolted from a bush
A merlin hovered in suspense
Beneath our feet were crimson stones
And here and there lay agates

How the soul is chained to time
And the guilt of experience
As beneath a quartz sky
We wandered with our vanity

An iron summer dust was
Sleeping on the printless ground
With its purple minerals and
The glitter of a faithless world

From that pausing afternoon
There was nothing elusive
Transfigured by the warm light
We stood above the turning plain

All our patience drew us
To that lonely focal spot
From one great periphery
We had circled for a life

Upon the body of the year
The texture of a soul is traced
Repeatedly our hearts are
Made perfect by that reflex

It was as if our footsteps
Were expunged from that point
And from that moment onwards
We could walk without fault

Granted life by the distance
Viewed apart from time
Beneath us the vision moved
With a semblance of unknowing
From the black hills to the ocean

I – 5 8

As we walked out one evening
Leaving tracks upon the sand
Our steps were soon overlaid
With marks of foxes and of birds

It is genius which makes us see
Offering us a vision where
We observe those ancient beings
Who barely watch our passing ways

They honour us with their feet
As they cross the blank-white earth
Gathering at the frontiers
Where humanity stands at a threshold

Quail and partridge rise at dusk
As drums and bells are sounded
The universe reveals its fire
With soft flame and vermilion smoke

As we walked out one evening
The land was still at rest
Birds cried and fields were sombre
No humanity was working

We crossed the empty distance
Pausing beneath quiet trees
Whose soft reserve satisfied
Our eyes from the sun's glare

Who knows where we are going
For time has no one point
We continue and we forget
So much suffering and joy

Genius rises from attachment
Speaking from beyond itself
Moving further than a life
Its words possess no single body

As we walked out that evening
Covered by obscurity
There was a fluttering in the air
As if the stars were being loosed

Then the land exposed its face
Standing on the ancient dust
Admiring earth's first columns
Its meteors and fragments

I – 5 9

IN a low grey luminous light
Along the coast in shining air
When the tide retreated leaving
Sands glistening and bare for miles
Some flamingoes passed overhead

They curved about and turned away
Undistracted in their intent
Gracious with a slow movement
Perfect in formation and tempo
As they winged the lucid emptiness

Their delicate quiet silence
Sublime with disregard
As the ocean turned and folded
Breaking open and retreating
The birds passed on and disappeared

One pure spot of dazzling colour
Upon a monochrome evening
Loveliness and equanimity joined
Avoiding human experience
In their solitary unmarked way
Untroubled by our presence

Along the shore and whitening sky
As a tide broke heavy and disordered
The sands reflected a blue heaven
Filmed by a receding ocean

Standing apart in isolation
Far from life or any movement
A crowd of tall serene flamingoes
Browsed upon shimmering pools

Brilliant in their pink apparel
As if pausing from another world
Exquisite in their unconcern
Careless of human loneliness

Suddenly rising to the air
In long and gracious strokes
They glided off down the wind
Seaward and disappeared

Such beauty is not for this time
Unearthly and super-natural
The flamingoes vanished from our sight
Too strangely perfect to remain
Upon this desolate vacant coast

I – 6 0

AMONG the pillars of the world
Hidden behind obvious displays
The guardians of our lives reside
Awaiting accomplishment and love

It is the fragrance of emptiness
That makes us see ourselves
A loneliness that aches always
Craving recognition in time

This living presence of duration
Where a heart's disquiet finds calm
Above the mountain birds pause
Hanging on the wind's fluency

Above the plain there is a fire
Burning openly in space
Emitting heat that gives time force
And blood that makes love wet

Streaming with this liberal passion
The fire dies and then returns
Copulating with itself the flames
Are made of jackals and of leopards

From the summit looking out
Our lives appear in apparition
As we walk the earth and disappear
When the guardians call our name

Once when the earth was slow
We walked openly and unconfined
Sun and moon would show their beauty
Keeping us within their bounds

Then we were strong with easiness
Saw men and women of the world
Going as if they simply possessed
Time with festival content

For solitude has no place
There is no light to solitude
True solitude is without person
Alone without name or body

So versatile and sensitive it
Cannot discern one thing
Solitude does not forget
For it has no memory

It is the keeper of our soul
Compassionate unspeaking
Watching for our indiscretion
When we forget ourselves

I – 61

ON my fifty-fifth year on earth
I walked out at Pragsar
Beside the lake and crimson hills
To observe the many birds

It had been lightly raining
The land was transient green
The sky unusually sapphire
With a border of white

Flocks of young grey herons
Dashed across the air
As pairs of kingfishers paused
Above the celadon water

I thought of the sea and coast
So present in my youth
As we gently crossed that plain
In order to look out

For this day the first sails
Had appeared far at sea
Small brown triangles bending
Low upon the horizon

As we approached the high rocks
A panther with her cubs
Gently slipped away as if
She did not need to exist

This had once been panther country
Long ago in the clear past
Now there was pure silence
And a sweetness to the air

At a shrine upon the plain
A man and woman prayed
Pouring milk upon a stone
As they offered up their bodies

So much in life disappears
As does time itself
And we are left gazing
Inwardly away from the world

Sea panther time stone
Conflate as they retreat
As if we are without efficacy
And nothing remains of the soul

Perhaps it is an envelope
Which we merely inhabit
Maintaining us with sensation
Making us sensitive

Staring out over Pragsar
Trying to discern the future
A tide was about to turn
Towards a nameless ocean

My wife sons central art
Long years of slowly walking
How the soul migrates through time
Yet is completely unknowing

Now this terrain inhabits me
Its earth is in my heart
Its unseen beneficence
Brings me to rest

Tall storks drifted overhead
Desultory kites glided
Cranes on extended wings
Circled down toward the water

Like birds going on the air
We leave no sensible trace
Oscillating heaven and earth
The causes are beyond us

On my fifty-fifth year of breathing
As we stood upon that hill
Love showed me its possession
And whispered of its proof
The secrets of adherence
And the knowledge it assumes

for Pragmulji

I – 6 2

A CURTAIN is drawn downward
And eyelids gently close
Memory is overdrawn and sleep
Quietens a restless brain

Time has disappeared for us
The palace become an ideal
Upon the lake night descends
As brown water recedes

Statues fall sand is blown
Yet human dignity and kindness
Although they cannot incise stone
Etch the world ineradicably

A sun settles to a tawny desert
As within a shadowed courtyard
Dogs and children play noisily
Cries and voices that never fade

Have you seen the slight impression
Upon a pillow at evening
A sentient damp fragrance
That a soul leaves upon rising

So an age turns into light
Another language is exchanged
Humanity forgets its promise
The old order is unheard

Humility once ruled this land
Its goodness without effort
Where rising up with the dawn
Consciousness was amazed that
Life should wear such beauty

I – 6 3

THE voice of a falcon calls me away
To put aside all human effort
To leave this world alone and
Go out of time across the sands

There is no solitude on earth
That is our transparent mystery
If we are strong enough to give
Our love in exchange for vision

Who dares to surrender and
Walk barefoot among the stars
Who will sleep with dust and stone
Taking pleasure in the coldness

There is no life we can know
Where we might exceed ourselves
Untiring in the pursuit of
Being that does not exist

The rasping whistle of a raptor
As it skims above the trees
Vacancy and loneliness await
In the voice of that bird
Beauty proclaiming its only name

I – 6 4

THERE is a little painted boat
With a stone man for its crew
It never settles to any shore
And its cargo is the soul of life

In a frantic and undying wind
We stare at the sun a while
Then as the boat approaches we
Exchange our world for water

Friendship with its sharp fragrance
Among the orchard trees
Supplied us with a source of time
We loved and dwelled and reconceived

As the worthless painted boat appeared
To retrieve us from life
It was kindness given by the sun
That allowed us to meet on earth
And to pause for a while

I – 6 5

THE outward movement of a soul
Passing throughout space
Ideal in its affinity as
A king and queen are standing
Unspeakable and beautiful

Moving outward from their feet
Are the ways they have walked
Guarding the moral hours
The old tissue of human lore
Made perfect by devotion

This is an arrow we do not see
Passing the surface of days
We observe its moving shadow
Tension of its sharpness and
Oblivion the missile conveys

What is creativity
Or genesis of true love
Language spoken before time
Before the speech of birds
Before light was distinct

Sometimes the king and queen
Walk the days unobserved
Their joy and suffering unseen
Before they vanish from the world
As if this body had no bearing

How to speak their names and
Make the universe effective
To touch the hand of those
Who elected to be patient
Who made time true for us
Benign and so generous

for Priti Devi

I - 6 6

HERE on this nutmeg island
Lovely as a wreck of paradise
Where the gentle squalls pass
Lightly overhead and sprinkle
The ground with a moist spray

A vibrant windward ocean
Sends its breezes shoreward
To humming-birds and grackles
Who chatter all the day as
Sweet rainbows come and go

Here where balm of darkness
Black indigo of inky quiet
Is tuned by frogs and insects
And foam sifting on the reef
Waves unfold - breaking open

Where admirals are all dead
And the captains deceased
The great ships disappeared
And stone walls collapsed
Iron become a green rust

Here on this volcanic isle
Of clove trees and pepper
Where vast oceanic swells
Rebound and flow backward
From bare sandy littorals

Where frigate-birds are soaring
And women carry broad knives
The men dive for shells and
Sometimes hunt small whales
From narrow-rigged canoes

Here where liquid fireflies
Splash their yellow fluid
Bursting softly and vibrating
Like orange drops of flame
Nocturnal and gleaming

Here in fragrant darkness
As ocean booms and shudders
Flexing in its currents and
Shifting listless vagrant moods
Unimpassioned unrelaxing

Here human consciousness
Is ever static and unmoving
As all a world scintillates
Rich in unseen potence like
Sulphur orchids in the mountains

All is patience here and tincture
Nothing ever is distinct
Merging humid unaffected
Like owls and mosquitoes
Unobserved invisible

At night ships ride on anchor
Hovering on a viscid swell
Near the susurrating reef
Their lights glow like suave eyes
As if existence were not full

Sometimes the air implodes
Soundless in the rhythmic night
On an empty blissful sea
Where storms flourish in suspense
Alone from terrestrial life

Monsoon oleander skies
Hours of slow terrific rain
An intense blood-heat dampness
Creates a redolent corrosion
Light cracks and sparkles sharply

It is the ephemeral that makes
Life beautiful in this place
That we might be witness
And time not be futile so
We can possess a little more

Here the days are vast and pure
The surf tinged electrically
Startling and covert white
As clouds like giant beings skim
Somnolent benign and tedious

Here where aging sailing ships
Fix their moorings to the coral
Where languid ospreys float
And palm trees are decaying
As shipwrecks sway innumerable

Here where dead sailors sleep
Beneath smooth mildewed stones
In their calm blank sea-graves
Beneath plantains and acacia
Where the termites make their home

Where the naked shipwrights build
Their new and polished vessels
Bending planks and caulking hulls
Cutting their strong ribs whole
As wives stitch prayers and sails

Sea-wives with green vivid eyes
And blond-almond tattooed skin
Perfumed with oil of grenadine
Wearing coloured asian cotton
With thick crude iron bracelets

Where flaws of a caressing wind
Are superficial to the touch
For the sea does not respond
And fish are oblivious to
Hurricanes that swing about

In this ginger tamarind land
Of lizard and of anaconda
Smoke moves slack and negligent
Like uncoiling time itself
To contract and expand at will

Only a present obtains here
Without reference or migration
The feminine leaves no trace
And the male holds no power
Nor claim to genealogy

The fragile vigour of the air
A coruscating sheer horizon
Where a scented placid landscape
With indolent fertility
Cloys senseless frangipani noon

Where life is prolific and
No thing becomes redundant
Birds are like a flickering
Of vital sentient ideas and
Constellations are unobserved

Here the women meet their men
In a low pink leafy dusk
As their sweat drips like milk
With odours of lime and rum
They fall asleep exhausted

Where youths pray each twilight
To the supernatural forces
Who live on hills and peaks
And girls wash in the morning
Importunate of conception

Their lust is like a sap or juice
Like a sea rich with crustacea
Or waves throwing out detritus
Or mahogany trees on fire
Torn with the weight of fruit

Where the centipedes and ants
Live in ease and desuetude
A gibbous moon their deity as
Among the flamboyant trees
They live and die unaware

Where cisterns and slimy wells
Send out small bats at dusk
Whose private mental lamps
Let them brush against the hair
Of those who walk in solitude

In the woodland of macaws
Swift noisy parakeets
Dash and flit and brashly scream
As they play on fecund vines
And small brown snakes are quiet

Our ankles in a warm sea-foam
As we walk among the ruins
All a world becomes unlived
Rapacious without motion
On this shining candid coast

An immense marine amplitude
With its ancient bleached jetsam
Where barracuda run and leap
Like spikes of darting metal
A mirror-glass of instant flight

The brief barracuda songs
Of violence and destruction
Annihilation of their hero
Who died beyond the reef
Sinking away unlit unknown

Herons egrets kingfishers
Viridian and quick cuckoos
The orange-flashing parrots
Who retire as the sun falls down
In a sudden flare of tangerine

Personal and cosmic now
Our way upon a mineral edge
A hard grey narrow margin where
Sea and stone and bronze fuse
To merge in hot cyanine light

From the sensual trade wind
Unannounced and lenient we
Depart for a perpetual void
Where only ideas survive
Always seeking knowledge

As pelicans glide to further isles
Rays shoot upward from the sun
Main and genoa are sheeted in
The vessel puts out from a cove
Entering the turbulence of streams

Sometimes we change our shape
Are seen to recommence
With endeavour and complexity
We resume and recur - the same
As we refine our vision

Sea-bones sea-wreckage all
Remorselessly rejected
Upon a carious rotten coast
Turning to fine sea-powder
For curving barren mangrove roots

This smooth damp rim of earth
Forever without exertion
Where sweat runs down and gathers
On a moist silvery lip stained
With turmeric and vanilla

Through saline coriander skies
Meteors fall like sullen planets
In apricot and turquoise evening
Cerulean clouds reveal their core
As sea and ocean clash and meet

When our ship weighs anchor
Jib and staysail drawn tight
The boat gently takes a course
Hesitating as we cross the flood
To go and meet with extinction

A serum-coloured plosiveness
Of low and seamless dawn
Where the islands turn cerise
As instantly the sloops tack out
Heading windward once again

Who shall weigh our souls
When the sun retreats forever
When the compass never points
And the bays are unremarked
Who shall patrol these islands

Under the measure of a fan
Whose rotors cool a room -
Deep motors thrum far away
To navigate an opulent depth
Of the gigantic unperceived

As the form of waves travel
Extending throughout time
So the ephemeral shall cause
Beauty to reside on earth
Incessantly and lightly transient
As we are kind and just in love

for Gregory Kallimanopoulos

I – 6 7

THERE where the sea brooded and roared
That in ecstasy rolls back
And throws itself repeatedly
Threshing the sand for a single truth

Dawn slight blue before light becomes
Visible and mild to human eyes
With distant lights of other islands
And far-off lamps of passing ships

Stepped hills appear and trees
And a grey-mercury reeling ocean
All the fiction of the earth - images
That we hold close to ourselves

Then desire begins to swerve -
Ulesses wakening seeks his wife
Caressing her about the hips
As they lie naked in the world

He heard the vivid squalls passing
Drumming hands on their zinc roof
And dozing in and out of sleep
He moved closer alongside Kiki

The indifference of unmoving Kiki
As she listened to the sea
Prolific and profuse it seethed
Reaching withdrawing repeatedly

Gone were the lost mornings when
She would yield all her desire
To luxuriate in her husband's passion
Those nights were no longer young

Near to their little teak-wood house
Small coffee-coloured cows browsed
Along the black sand of the shore
White egrets perched upon their flanks

She could smell the first smoke
Of day - odour of dung and grass
And hear a thudding of boats
Noisily speeding across the swells

A kingfisher chattered as it flew
Across the bay beneath their land
As lunar shadows were stretching out
Upon the ground in tedious shapes

Small anacondas coiled and knotted
The forest dripped with sweet rain
Smoke hung acrid on leaves and air
Green-throated colibris and blossom

She could hear the first motors
As boats dashed out towards the fields
Doves and grackles pattered upon
The railings of their terrace

The spray and boom of the sea
A final scattering of bats
Mosquitoes hungry for human blood
Before the day caused them to vanish

All these sounds reached Kiki's ears
As she lay still so as not to rouse
Her husband from the renewed sleep
To which he had once more descended

So many years she had waited for him -
Ulesses working on the ships
She never imagined a marriage defunct
That happiness could be so abandoned

Another squall raced down from hills
Speckling the corrugated metal roof
Then rushing slow explosions came
Of deep-grey pelting rainfall

The couple rested on a thin bed
While black tarpon curled through the bay
Arcing in perfect symmetry
Herding a shoal of darting fish

She loved her husband - but now
His mood was speechless flint
These days they scarcely spoke
Shared food together and casual loving

She knew her devotion to be enduring
And like the rose of dawn he would
Always be there to accept her need
But life had become an attendant waiting

She loved Ulesses for his wandering reason
He had left the isle and returned
Knew seas and iron islands and cities
Habits and knowledge - the skill of others

Yet Kiki knew the magia of summons
Was familiar with spectral figures
Who appeared when her eyes were closed -
As fish touch a seam of water

No longer capricious but clairvoyant
Kiki adored that limbo world
Something she never admitted
Never mentioned to her husband

His body smelled of salt and leaves
Of bread and oil - Ulesses
This man who had once so ruled
Every second of her days

Like an old cutlass now he was
That hung upon a wall and rusted
But their bound oaths of long ago
Remained perpetual for her

There was a sound of pistons revving
Of plywood hulls striking waves
A cry of male voices calling
Telling boats where the tarpon waited

'What light shall burn away the suffering
Of painful grieving humanity
What daring can release us' she mused
'From so much pity and duress

This man I once imagined as
The perfect sum of all that breathed
I gave myself to him because
He wanted me so much

To me he taught compassion and
The timelessness of human spirit
His foresight and accuracy
Were for me more than life'

Through the doorway she could see
Rosy tips and strands of dawn
Could hear the ferry's engines humming
Entering the bay it slowed its pace

'This is the smallest day' - Ulesses
Had said as they retired last night
'The sun is standing now and soon
Will move backward on the horizon north

Like glossy planets in the sky at dusk
When the ghostly sea pauses
As insects and gliding birds test
The flashing and shining darkness

Then I know that soon we could
Be easily walking out of time
Into the light beyond the hills
Beyond the ocean's ancient sounding'

Kiki withdrew from bed and went
To stroll the grounds of their pasture
Watching the sea listening waiting
For new promises to break her doubt

A rimmed moon extinguished itself
Among dense marine clouds
As the first pelicans swung on the air
She thought of her sleeping husband

Untimed impersonal careless
Yet whole and benign - the vastness
Of nocturnal trade-wind soothed her
Its glittering heaven and sheer air

Days were blurred and weightless now
Fused and simply indistinct
They were like her grey-eyed husband
Pensive and involved of evening

She was so tentative and Ulesses
So male and made of bones
But no one lived in her amber eyes
Her soul was always ranging elsewhere

It was Ulesses who gave her place
Stature and torso that she could hold
And when he lay between her legs
She thrilled with her body's issue

'Sometimes my soul goes to a dancing place
And alone and quite free
It plays and turns and watches there
Yet soul has no memory – like Ulesses

How all of life takes from us
Some days more some days less
Each dawn measures and subtracts
Reducing us as it rushes away

The irony and paradox of life
Which only love can combat
Love keeps our diminution
From removing us from this earth

The world is animate and true
And we - a tissue-globe of thought
One forceful the other insubstantial
And that is all that we can say

Love gives us tongues and insight
It fills us with concupiscence
Without love we are empty creatures
Phantoms who cannot speak nor touch

His voice removed my loneliness
Just as his strength took my lust
In his person I find a home
And in his sleep I find rest

He is my snake and fruit-tree
He is the child I envisage
And during the insensible night
He is the glow that reveals a man'

A bright pink dawn was rising
And insects swarmed like birds
And as the blue sea played turquoise
A white and molten moon was green

The inside of her thighs were still
Wet from the hours before
When Ulesses had woken at midnight
Compelling her satisfaction

His scent and tang was on her skin
Her hair still tangled by
His passion and taut urgence
A smell of kisses stayed in her mouth

'True solitude' he had once said
'Occurs when the most restless element
Of a man's need to forget
Comes to rest in a woman's arms'

He would always remain her match
Even if gravity and reserve
Made her discount a first tenderness
During the time when they were young

Sea-grape and coco-palm nodded
As she looked out from the railing
Recalling the anguish of his manner
When he had fallen asleep last night

Kiki stood by her garden beside
The datura and okra and sorrel bush
Something in her longed to weep
Some unspeakable desperation

Trees leopard-coloured in the dark
The moon ringed with tortoise-shell
Under a net Ulesses lay sighing
And she longed for him and wept

'Gone is the golden age when love
Was complete and men and women
Found neither emptiness nor despair
When vision was love's phase and source

Now my unbearable soul is craving
And my husband is not a man
But a piece of cloth and a few buttons
Like a fish with nothing to say

Coco-palm' she said grasping the tree
'I planted you when we married
Now you grow and fruit and shake
And I am alone with a man's misery'

She could hear the spiralling cry
Of cockerels' voices in the village
The listless bark of a dog and
A bristling of night's last darkness

'He dances in his masks and I
Dance in mine and at times
The music turns and we pass on the floor
And sometimes our masks are the same

That is all that love achieves
A spontaneous recognition of person
Features we wear in our oblivion
When soul possesses no view of its own'

'I bear a great love for this place
But I know of no loyalty to location
I have only my love for you' he had said
'And I fear to lose this island

Despond and remorse give us hope
For without love we are void
Silence is the most complete space
For those who have no home'

'Have I wasted my youth' she thought
'Become another's courtesy
Body whom he takes to himself
When he needs to lose his life

The axle of our lives is hidden
We see the moon and sun and think
Yes - this is how we turn
Yet there is no turning of love's wheel'

Once his solitude had drawn her
But now his reticence was exceeding
It was as if he were captive
To an idea or lost experience

She loved to walk the grounds
During night when the stars shot
And crackled overhead and the moon
Was luminous on the ocean's surge

In a shadowy stainless blackness
The passing and responsive flutterings
Rustling and footfall – all these
Were familiar powers to Kiki's mastery

On the mountain-side nearby
An upright tall stone chimney
Of the old lime factory stood
Perpendicular and guardian

Among many ruined citrus trees
And thorny bougainvillea bushes
The genius of time - flawed and unfirm
Was like her husband's dreaming

'How to love a man who is not there
To watch him tap his barometer
And stand before a wooden idol
His hands folded in prayer'

A meteor scorched and burned a track
Sparking downward from the sky
She knew she must return to him
For often at dawn he needed her

Snakes bats fireflies these
Were her muted companions
Goats sheep dogs cattle
The donkeys fowl and the apparitions

As she walked back up to the house
Masses of small brown mosquitoes
Touched and ran against her face
Her feet slipping in the rain

She loved the saline wind at night
Its sugary smoky warmth and how
It rushed upon her and against the sea
Driving waves onto sandstone rocks

Curling back towards the bed
Beneath the silky net - she moved
Beside her husband whose immobility
In the darkness amazed her

That day she would have to walk
Across the isle for a wedding
In the boatyard where her godson
Was to accept a blonde-eyed girl

She heard the weekly tanker drop
Its bronze anchor to the bay
Ready to receive vessels whose engines
Needed fuel and news from the isles

She recalled how she and Ulesses met
He had seduced her with tales
Of other domains hardship and people
She had been caught in his storied web

'You are my ship called *Patience*
With your green mascara and azure glances
Where youth and beauty mix like the sea
In a happy mist of mutual pleasure'

The powdery jasmine-coloured sky
Coral and blue of alto-cirrus
An oval moon occluded by cloud
As they walked home from the bar that night

Kiki - solemn and distressed now
They slept on the veranda of the house
Wanting so much the love of her husband
Yet tired of his habitual embrace

Once he had laughed so much with her
They had walked the island for miles
She had shown him all the paths
The sandy coves bays and caverns

They had loved so much in those years
Their ardour inhabited the isle
Now their kisses were performed
Enacted without detail

Yet she loved this turbulent surly man
His words were the walls of her heart
To her he was as much a presence
As the landscape of these shores

Day released its milky haze
A humid blur of waves and light
A quiet plosive rush of marine
Forever smoothing and filling the rocks

Like an octopus explodes to blackness
With a sudden discharge of fear
So Kiki dropped her shift to the floor
Slipped easily beside her naked man

He was awake and touched her breasts
She sensed his fervent movement
Then he was upon her and inside
And she forgot her disillusion

As the sea crumpled on the shore
As iguanas rhythmically shook their heads
As the coco-palm quivered with breeze
So Kiki felt her life return

Her soul – like forest amaryllis
Rose upward and opened out its leaves
As humming-birds hovered and alighted
A candescent heat imbued her blood

His estranged soul approached at last
Its vibration rose in her tissue and cells
Her body stirred like the ocean stirring
And with a final exhalation she cried

All the pain loneliness and sorrow
Experience that possessed no word
Disappeared as his body rose and fell
And the implacable man she loved returned

As her husband exclaimed his joy
And his limbs carefully relaxed
Kiki felt his shoulder muscles
His fatigue and weariness loosely soften
Each of them murmured the other's name

I - 6 8

YOU wakening in your soft white net
Smelling of sleep and sweet grapefruit
I long to taste your lips and drink
The water only you possess

I love you for your body's light
You are my motive being and rest
Vivacious deliquescent you
Are the spirit of my new woman

I love your candid solitude
The way you walk along the shore
Never swerving like the wind
Completely like the darkness

I love your pity for all kind
The trust you have for human speech
Compassionate with affection you
Apprehend love's transparency

I love your sensuous liberty
The way you do not recall
I observe no consciousness
Without your true compulsion

You are the pain when I am beaten
Replete with all anxiety
On double wings of grief I rise
Toward your singular estate

Beautiful and soothing you
Are like a young traveller's tree
Within a subtlety of shadow
You know how it is to love

You expose to me love's tissue
So my thirst becomes fluid
All that runs upon your tongue
About the smallness of your torso

Citron-trees with wrens and swallows
Entangled in your topaz vision
Revealing and mnemonic you
Are my perfect absolution

I love your ideal gentleness
Equilibrium of your wealth
Yet how I suffer and endure
For my experience of you

Like an octopus or starfish
Or an iridescent dolphin
Something lucid in your eyes
Is never quiet nor still

Agile mobile unhesitating
As we move together coupled
Two bloods flowing uniform
I hear the ocean in your voice

A pang I feel throughout this life
Not being wholly at your side
With you in my arms I am
United and so universal

Briefly I borrow you in time
Glimpsing through your living form
Yet earthly vigilance is weak
And you evapourate

The moon is settling into waves
And admiring her recession
You are the tawny bird whom
I touch with slow desire

Mistress of my patience you
Stand upon the many hours
Like uprising cumuli
You come and go upon me

In my mouth I taste your flesh
Your slightness and vitality
I love the slippery sensitive
Currency of your passion

My leeward and my windward place
Trade wind of all existence
You are my three-masted boat
Dare I name and announce
You mirror of the invisible

I – 6 9

IT is not what we leave
But what we go towards
That counts in the end
For nothing is ever still
There is no unmoving
In each other's eyes
We only breathe and dwell

Accomplishment is nil
If it does not send us on
Toward what we do not
Know or cannot gain
For nothing is ever lost
In our recollection

Indifferent are those runners
The foretellers of time
Who – sleeping on the earth
Await red morning light

As they crouch about a fire
Whose small flames of thornwood
Reach into black air
One or two quietly sing –

'Inanimate the sky and
Immanent the universe
Yet inevitable our end
Soon we are all invisible
And creativity and affection
Will never have even moved'

I I - 1

I LIKE to watch you walk
And count the rings I never see
Yet how unbearable it is
Not giving to the one we love

Deft visceral autonomous gifts
Of time as years dilate
In my despair I visit paradise
None of the birds notice me

Swan geese heron gull
Their world is out of time
Desperation drove me there
Beyond the present circles

I was pleased not to exist
They did not see my soul
Pleased to vanish in this way
Disappearing inside heaven

Only love draws us back
When we are only giving
I love to watch you moving
Especially when you are alone

I I - 2

THE end that is always to come
But is only anticipated
Where does destiny begin
In what day or moment

Or in a well-loved promise
Is it fulfilled so simply
Does the presence of the wind
Affect living sentience

Fragrance of a human body
Enigma of human beauty
What is it we do not have
Which is so dispossessing

Being drawn by the not-having
And then in the satisfaction
We still miss the conclusion
To this long endless call

I I - 3

THERE are two windows in this life
Through which quiet observers stare
One looks to the moral universe
And its immutable sky

The other turns within to where
Lovers meet in brief white fire
Becoming an insensible one
Where they might lose themselves

Between these transparent panes
Truth like flirtation passes
Involving eyes and hearts and
Hands that long to touch forever

Some in darkness live and grieve
Desperate for a single view
Of justice in reflection where
All that came before occurred

I I – 4

STAY hawk – there is no descent
There is only one day ever
In our lives and one occasion
For vision to be complete

Be unlike a dagger falling
Cutting the sacrificed year
Separating yellow light
From noon and zenith

Make no descent with
Red blades slanting and
Without a cry reveal
Voices hidden in the wheat

True places do not occur
Except in your heart
Among fresh leaves oscillating
Or footsteps receding from life

Glide away into grey air
Without wheeling and keep
Your horizon from igneous
Ancient unbearable grief

Stay high on summer and tower
Be the genius of birds
Proclaiming our promise
True sky and true curving stars

Stay and never incline
To our one small day and night
Be among the circling hours
Our sharply human axle burning

I I - 5

NOW the sacred geese advance
In varying line southward
Across the coast and isles
The rocks tides currents sand

As crimson leaves descend so
The birds depart this world
Rivers cool and life sleeps
In a quiet onset of darkness

What mariners now put out
With small wooden sailing vessels
Going toward an horizon where
Solitude and emptiness are all

Humming-birds heron swans
Vanish into a lowering sky
As the air becomes cold and
All earthly light diminishes

A candid moon moves to circle
As dry hills become unstable
Grass and reeds fall down now
In this vast soundless demise

So many rings of shadow
That dance above our sleep
It is as if we are initiates
Into a secret of renewal

Hammers of wisdom in the heart
Formless and without dimension
Drive us toward one truth
Both weightless and transparent

I I - 6

UNDER Polaris darkness spins
Rotates so invisibly
We cannot see this movement yet
Our constancy is perpetually moved

A golden rain of carnal joy
The silent pressure of the stars
Commit us to live in time
As days are circled round by years

The stiff knuckles of a hawk
Reddened by the blood of winter
Its beak raw and sharp with
Fragments of hardened snow

The bird surveys mortality
From soundless frozen air
No cry nor voice is ever heard
In this defeat of animal warmth

Like a meteor it falls down
Or like a comet's wake
The bird having sighted life
Strikes – exchanging souls

Midwinter as a grey sun pauses
Hovering above white distance
The hungry raptor oversees
This low motionless terrain

Winter with its rain and ice
Small dense uncoloured days
How we promise to be true
As we struggle on the plain

The thin bare wind of winter
Sterile and unnourished
Blows across bones and hills
Without residence on earth

Fields are now transfixed by frost
Where slight footprints pass
Telling of their solitude
And of mute desperation

This is no worldly triumph
For only sleep is possible
Consciously the sky flares
At night beneath the hunting stars

Years like leaves are threshed
Shaken by the wind
Beneath a milky zenith and
Profane scabbard of life

Under Polaris light stays
Poised faithful and firm
We break our hearts with pathos
Yet fidelity is possible on earth

For there is victory even
In the weightless bird we glimpsed
In our words and affection
Giving ourselves away

TONIGHT as a dead wind blows
And the dark lakes crack and
The unseen black river stiffens
I wish that you were in my arms

I wish that you came to my bed
And with kindness offered
Your admiration and with you
Without conscience I slept

If I called you here now
Would you approach and lightly
We could be perfectly without
Pretence or any disturbance

If you were in my arms now
Our understanding of the world
Might vanish in mutual symmetry
Leaving us simply believing

Yet the adverse wind blows
These slow hours are insufficient
For you sleep far away content
Unaware of how life could rest

Bare trees creak and scrape
No one bird nor small animal
Survives the absolute cold
Only love continues burning

So I summon you now
Pretending to say your name
When this emptiness resounds
Making quietness so impersonal

For your heart is not beneath
My warm hand and no one
Is afoot on earth tonight
Except for solitary darkness

I I - 8

THE luminous paramour who has no body
No name and speaks no word and knows
How it is to be human circling us
When we are still quiet in the world

Morning like an unseen raptor
With its hard blade of shadow
Falls on our deficient minutes
And our wounds of indecision

Then the flames surround us
Clear lucid invisible fire
As each quick day vanishes
In haste as if hunted by hawks

In this seasonal flamboyance
We are stripped of all clothing
Ingenious hands barely touch
Blameless and sincere

Superhuman are those hours
With eyes gently closing
They judge us for our kindness
Our attention to their light

Exhilaration runs on the air
Knowing there is only innocence
Cruel and separating lovers
Shining severely as they embrace

Beneath a heavenly universe
Stars pause each vivid second
Their secrecy of truth is just
A friend with whom we walk

Miraculous like nothing on earth
This companion who takes us away
With the moral beauty of courtship
Deluding us of absence

For supernatural is this life
Unspeakably loyal and so inviting
Regardless of how we pretend
We are here for ever

All creation now observes
This secret of true love
We enter the world but are prior to life
As sunlight enters each following day

I I – 9

BESIDE a grey-green lake
Beneath a livid sunless sky
You and I walked once
Recalling our years together

Within the surrounding forest
So many lives were watching
Staring at us speechless
Admiring our old friendship

As the powder in a shell
Knows nothing of the world
So we in our affection
Ignored so much life

Snow has now silenced
The water and the trees
Deadened all the roads
Hiding every footstep

Without amity in life
We cannot exist and yet
If we do not admit
To human suffering we fail

The desire to end desire
Is not desire but passion
Indifferent to ideals and
Refusal to be faithless -

Light intercepted by
The beauty of a living body
So we become aware
How shadow changes shape

All night the twanging ice
All day a birdless blue air
Water beneath the surface
So still as to be eternal

Grey ice in thick plates
Broken and dispersed onshore
How we built a column of pieces
An infinite pillar we adored

On the lake a shell breaks
No one hears a sound
So in our humanity
We betray all admission
Our hope the dust of stars

I I – 1 O

ALL victory can be broken
By the great extent of solitude
Loneliness will crush happiness
Leaving mastery alone

The sun our only vessel can
Founder upon despair
Both personal and universal
Random captious haste

My ancestral man who
Has walked ten thousand years
Who simply stands and waits
Regardless of time going

Observing us but unaware
That we are his far-children
Spawned by his old lust or
What became a slow loving

Tired of only weeping in
This watery acumen of days
How is it we are separate
When we are in fact the same

Stone copper wood bones
Which first gave you music
Flutes and songs remade
From the shoulder of a bird

There is no earthly purchase
But a long courageous going
From life to life in circles
Where the sun sings its journey

A beautiful sleek torso
Of a creature lost in shadow
The eternal object of a song
With its own sufficient instant

Sunlight proclaims our destiny
Omits the moral darkness
The uncommon and so evasive
World where we are confined

Girls among the green wheat
Young men lying by a river
All the animate world is so
Determined by this symmetry

No bird crosses the cold air
No fish moves beneath the ice
No voice happiness nor expression
Comes between sky and ground

Vulnerable and so fragile
We walk ten thousand centuries
The lakes remain and the rocks
There is no mortal treasure

Yet trees are dressed in light
Young animals upon their boughs
And gifts of truth are hidden
In slight acts of compassion

We must believe our goodness
For that is all our time is worth
Let us renew our promise so
Kindness treads a flat terrain

I I - 11

FRAGRANCE of low evening sky
Brazen sunlight glancing down
Breathless owls glide toward
A cold and lifeless forest

Beauty of a nude figure
Walking on deserted land
A true man and true wife
Joined by abounding nature

We cannot dismiss the world
Because it is not solemn
For the universe does not
Accept a moral force in life

There is no judgement
Inhabiting an austere sky
When the lions stand about
Waiting for us to speak

For the envelopes they bring
To be simply opened and
Thousands of many years
Will vanish in that second

As we walked upon a frozen lake
Grey air fog and creaking
Where the waters began to split
And gelid leaves decay -

I told the sea beneath our feet
A secret we had kept
As long as youth and beauty last
We are caught by a thread

I told our secret to the sea
To the grass and fields of sand
How days are not days upon
The tense membrane of time

Into a shimmering darkness
Running with music and light
I told the ancient coastal air
Of what we could not say

Beneath the powdered stars
Only the soul is real
A small luminous circle
Suspended between sky and water

This is a perfect work
Above all that is
The mower with stone and blade
Who never desists from labour

If the spirit is alive then
A lost soul is a ghost
Phosphoros speeding in the night
A heart driving toward its mate

How can we match time
With so much uncertainty
Indelible and lucid passion
Set in a world of cavities

I know my love for you
Is less than your worth
But I long for that moment
When our desire is equal

Paradox or dilemma
Like water we may not drink
Yet my thirst is not fluid
Just as the stars do not speak

I know my love for you
As a light that moves always
Towards the shade and yet
We never touch nor stay

So much new water
Running through our blood
Renewing life's motive
Always transporting us

Fluctuation of the river
Its eyeless sweeping heaven
A sun that never pauses
As if sleeping on the wing

Then your hands reach down
Entering the heart
A place no one mentions
Where we were once founded

Now as I take myself
To the room where you reside
Where I say your name
May my words be acceptable
As grain hidden in the wheat

I I – 1 2

GEESE circling in wide arcs
Above a frozen lake
As evening reclines upon
Grasses and brown reed

Beside this crimson water
Trees are black and aged
As shadows rise upward
Toward the gathering birds

Frost snow ice mist
Hail wind and thunder
The fluency of the sky
Moves like a slow broad river

We walk on earth a brief while
Accomplishing our words
Ascending and descending
As if a strange rare speech

Like years these archaic birds
Come and go and re-appear
With their streaming speech
Dissolve mundane experience

I have seen the geese gather
Upon the stiff dry earth
Dark wings resting upon rushes
Beside the river in early spring

In rain fugitive from wind
The air noisy and disturbed
I have heard them closely singing
Unsheathed - stripped of frailty

Calling all the universe
With commonplace humility
Their solemn careful sound
Is witness of no aspiration

Such music is unspeakable
Becoming distant and unheard
Despite our indecency and
Dilemmas of enduring grief

This vision of acoustic life
As a cold river runs coastward
And magnolia forsythia crocus
Colour small resolute days

Inevitable and unfamiliar
Infinitely continuous
Between diaphragm and heart
All the world is going

There are no leaves upon the trees
No courtship nor contest of life
No blood exposed nor incited
Being far removed from this hour

As the year dies and then reforms
Crossing between time and light
In the temperament of their song
We forget anguish or ambition

Friction of language and dust
Where so much is crucified each day
In the beauty of the birds' singing
Suffering does not compromise
We benefit from their praise

11 – 13

WHO are you lying there
Asleep on the snow
So invincible once
King or queen of the air

Crimson bronze yet cold
Now stiff with ice and stone
Your heart remains perpetual
Gentle warm and fierce

The hiding of your mastery
Was the origin of our life
How you never suffered nor
Accepted earthly distress

How can mystery perish
What journey out of time
Is this that you have made
Descending from endless height

Once you held a mirror
Deep within your eyes
Looking down upon the universe
On every moving kind

A scabbard of affection
Whose fame is made of light
You oversaw our lives as
The wind caressed your body

Always innocent you were
Your beauty had no sheath
Like heaven at night gazing
Observing our progress

Sovereign beauty of the world
Without heart or repetition
Without days nights or years
You are infinitely enduring

Always present in the distance
Observing us with compassion
You are the only one and
So we adore your ways

In the slim fissure between
Sea and reddening sky
Your body is revealed to us
And then time is transformed

There is no horizon now
As fiery dancers undulate
On a cold grey-blue ocean
Where we begin and end

Your face streams with spray
There is no grief only
The play and dive of white birds
Who escort you for ever

Those immutable forms
Of shadows on the land
Offer us our single freedom
To apprehend your bounds

Before kings and queens
All this had been foretold
There is no deception now
During swift footed darkness

11 – 14

IF memory unbecomes us
For submitting to no rule
We seek to emulate that way
By offering our desire

Footprints drying in the air
That approach and vanish
Perfume of lime trees that
Fills the night with volume

Foot-marks upon the earth
Where once a being passed
Haunting us with a shape
Not to be transformed

Where will they lead us to
And might we then return
If the experience is more
Than human vanity allows

11-15

LIKE a swallow you were
Precise in your kindness
Quick as you flew away
Into colourless morning

How the human spirit
Glides apart from the body
Soundless even without breath
Becoming absolute once more

Will the swallow find a house
In the ashes of a human soul
As a voice rises toward the sun
Saying - we are perfectly alone

Through the cracks of every rock
Where iris and crocus unfold
Beneath smooth wings of time
You shall make a new dwelling

In fragility honesty quietness
Poised in private devotion
Careful toward humanity
Who know nothing at all

Yet treasuring all modesty
Lucid as a flawless vessel
The integrity of a thousand years
Turned from a potter's hand

We each possess two destinies
In this world and beyond
And what we accomplish here
Attends us in the future

The beauty horror and the pity
As we go from room to room
Certain of immortality yet
Unsure of how it is we lived

If we could count our bones
What would they tell us
Of the vision we express
As we go so mysteriously

Where shall swallows settle
This spring as they dash north
In possession of no doubt
Keeping only to the light

Their honesty is that we see them
And sometimes hear a word
Even as they cross darkness
In complete silence saying -

We are perfectly alone and
That is our earthly joy
This is how true lovers give
Their promise back to life
Graciously returning

11 - 16

I DECK the house in flowers
A wreath for the door
A vase of barley for the table
Beside the bed some tissue poppies
Of the most intense of madder

Vine leaves for the chimney
Anemone for window jambs
One could continue so for ever
The gate - steps to the path
But there are ends

A garland for a roof post
And time will marry time
This ring which one makes - saying
This is where you are and were
And this was simply happy
Shared by those who form your thought

Remember - the rest is not
Possible to ever hold
Is impossible to covet
The colours go but not the point

I I – 1 7

SHE files her nails with the grace of a wren
Till they shine like a polished willow grove
And whilst she works her fingertips fine
He plays for her on his bamboo flute

Her eyes are as pure as the pearl skin of shells
Her limbs are like feathers adrift in the sea
For the joy of her beauty and flight of her voice
He plays to her on his bamboo flute

Her feet are unslippered and dance through the tide
Her dance for the moon is covered with leaves
As lightly she steps through sonorous waves
To the tuning of his bamboo flute

I I – 1 8

HERE they are panting teeth bared
With hazy eyes and slow steps
Bright red dogs without any sky
As the hills turn into powder

With a hiss of insects at noon and
Liquid torches of fireflies at night
On the river a slow green mist
Hangs opaque with humid odour

Dawns are turbid and smoulder
Flicker through dense foliage
Days wheel by with dull tension
As the dogs growl in the distance

The year hovers balanced
Guarded on either side
The tongue of the beast flashes
Light held tightly between iron paws

Soon the hounds will slowly
Be pacing home in the dusk
Along the terraces distributing
Their gold in the low red light

Are we vulnerable now - deceived
Without origin or possible fiction
The scarlet dogs hold up a mirror
Where our supposed unity vanishes

Hot fiery snarling with joy
The vermilion dogs of summer
The sky fuses in a blur of lead
And shadows snap at their edges

11-19

IF the pursuit of happiness
Portrays how it is that we
Apprehend the stillness of life
Not empty but perpetual

Now at this haying time
As a tall sun hovers
And a world gently pauses
Consumed by granular heat

Beneath a low shadow of cedar
Upon warm grey rocks
A girl and a boy say what
No one else on earth knows

Across the grass - under the leaves
As quick swallows perforate
Soft opaline dusty air
One word secures our pursuit

Despite the snarling cruelty
That inhabits so much time
Like a snake defining its grief
Or the walls we must overcome -

All our efforts to succeed
Cannot speak of what it is
That we harvest from our days
Beyond the captivation of love

I I – 2 O

How is it two people love
What is it they see
When in their silent prowling
They meet irresistibly as if
Ingenuous in matrimony
Like water as it touches grain
Or intimation of what drives
A man and woman to surrender
To the perfume of their nakedness
As in connubial light they are
Revealed and stripped bare of all
But their nature and its touch
So they might slightly witness
The genius of beauty hidden

There are swimmers in the sun
Or birds in a palace of wind
Who mirror perfectly desire
Making love transparent
Weightless and without cause
Becoming the first landscape
Rich with amorous passion
Their skins stained with saffron
Of both desire and death until
They disclose their liquid heart
Diminishing all suffering
Making this completely beautiful
Phenomenal and virtuous
Not mistaking dawn for noon

How long is a day if
It be hidden without light
Refulgent and attractive
Without scent of human breath
That immutable agency
When the loss of our perfection
Is more distressing than
Spiritual beauty vanishing
Just as a boy and girl attract
Each other and dominate the earth
Proclaiming thoughtlessness
Then launching into night
A vessel and casting thin sails
Where the wind can lean and press

Iridescent now is solitude
As the year hovers above zenith
When wanton light lives alone
Craving the company of darkness
Then lovers hold in their arms
All they might ever confess
For wheels are always circling
Never knowing of just release
That perfect man and woman
Who conceived the future twice
Mysterious and inseparable
They were consumed unbearably
Their solitude lightly unmade
As intimacy became discretion

11 – 21

GEESE landing upon a lake
In the final red bars of dusk
The soft noise of a hundred wings
Mowing through cool dark air

From over smooth hills they came
Crying out in long formation
Above a half-moon was gaping
At a brilliant white planet

Onto calm water descending
Something greater than we ever were
Rising and falling onto a lake
Circling low in black emptiness

Further off in a house children
Were imitating a tune
As the last thin pink rays went
From a primitive sky to another world

Reversal of so much human life
We repeat thinking we invent
Sleep fills our hemisphere as
An owl glides from its wood

I I – 2 2

A LION walks in the shade
The vine curls about a stem
The sun is stronger and brighter
Although the hours diminish

Evening will come soon as
A mower advances through light
A lilac-hyacinth sky is tinted
With subtle strands of pink

Broad long fields are being hayed
The air sweet with seeds and dust
Calmness as low shadows rest
All being presently still

A fawn is solitary in the woods
Fern and birch are wet from night
There is a sound of falling water
For hours from eaves to earth

There is a gentle passive murmur
Of rain upon slow waves
The ancestors have all departed
Gone up to the far mountains

They stare down at us in silence
At dusk as long days recede
Listening to streams running
A grey sound upon cold cedars

Pine-needles pollen feathers
Stones gather upon the floor
Spiders weave in the threshold
Wooden rooms are empty of time

Goodness and children and dogs
Small animals that inhabit this world
This low venerable isle of rock
All pause in strict lightness

On this finest day to heaven
Thank you dear friend for
The voice that you once gave us
Without which nothing exists

Like a bird flying at night
Soundless through dark air
All that life transfigures
Lacks recognition without amity

The lion walks in shadow
The hours though more intense
Rich with fullness are smaller
Diminished in their amplitude

Each cool damp dawn as
We walk beside this still blue lake
When leaves are fresh upon
Dust of a white limestone track -

No matter how much we suffer
Whatever ordeal and agony
By going just one second further
One fraction of an instant ahead -

Our vision will always succeed
Finding goodness in truth
So thank you for your bond
Your kindness and affection

Thank you for this world
For your companionship and
Happy places where we walked
For only you have made us love

The stillness of the house now
Of life and of hills and lake
Of geese cormorant sails and skies
As swallows thread the air
The harvest is taken in and stored

11 – 23

ON my sixty-sixth year on earth
I walked out for distraction
Loving the sand loving the dust
The unmasking of the air

A firm wind from off the lake
Was bevel on the hot light
As if desperate for release
For destiny to be complete

The distances were hazy and
The low brown hills at rest
As my years gathered close
Awaiting their dismissal

So much time so little place
So little achieved in living
Yet this is where my heart stays
Where I wish to sleep

Unknown unseen yet observant
Printless on this soft ground
No one on earth knows
How we are here nor why

The low green water of the lake
Where heron stood composed
Was perfect in its stillness
Untroubled by humanity

The dry flat plain extended
For invisible miles away
As among the thorns I walked
And at each step vanished

All of moral life and vision
Ordeals of simple human effort
Were less than this beauty
Without grief only promise

There was no oblivion here
And yet no awareness
A terrain of stone and powder
Of old mineral detritus

For one grain of consciousness
Is more victorious than any joy
This strong light-blue light
Luminous draws us elsewhere

Perfectly stationary as we wander
It supports all we know
Yet our feet do not touch
Its worldly genius of love

On my sixty-sixth year of time
Obedient to perpetuity
With hawks and lapwings
With the speed of kingfishers
In the light of truth there is no one

I I – 2 4

THE stainless mirror of awareness
Uncreated and so perfect
Cadence of a human pulse
Measuring the universe
Involving earthly time

Silvery and shining like
Fluid that is just alive
Motionless yet implying
All that moves for a while
For light compels us now

Our first freedom was like hay
In a quiet winter barn
Where intimate we held
All that we might need
Caught in summer's odour

The second freedom was in loving
Giving more than we received
The third was in watching
Becoming slow and beautiful
Like a river in the dark

The fourth freedom lay
Embedded in our lust
Inscribed at night by stars
Like moonlight on the snow
When nothing can be said
A vision we concealed

For no one understood
How long ago in youth
We crossed the fertile sea
Bitter waves of loneliness
Cold in a grey-green flood
Until we reached the rocks -
If we do not comprehend
Human suffering we
Cannot know this world

Between us and the sun
Only time survives
When on a sublime lake
We stared at the hills as
Truth stood on a mountain
Sanguine optimistic
Stripping us of falsehood

We became a girl in heart
A young man in his blood
A lioness walking on a plain
When the world slept

Those were our first rights
And beside a fire we shared
The stones we learned to cut
Where it was simply written
Stars and grass and love
Were only one and conscience
Could not be futile
As hand in hand through days
Our promises were kept

11 – 2 5

As bees are to pollen so
Are words to a bride
Undressing in darkness
Ancient children of night

Where blood enters blood
Without dust we become
Yet cannot outpace
One just moral pulse

Now every thin shadow
Is gently withdrawn
As we walk on a thousand
Previous grey hours

Thank you for midnight
Which allowed us to see
For loneliness that made
Us aware of the world

Thank you for anguish
Which gives us the vision
To grasp what is not
Known by a name

This light which bears us
In its weightless hands
So we barely exist -
There is joy in that

Seedless rootless
The source of life is fluent
And the bride and groom
Never rest from loving

11 – 26

THE ingenuity of the sky
That rules us with schemes
Corn wheat barley and
White dust upon bronze grain

Fields bleached by moonlight
Like marble statues in the dark
Owls and foxes hunt the night
Whilst deer feed on wet grass

Sheep are resting on the hills
As pheasant search at dusk
Young horses keep to shadows
Where boys tell stories

Monochrome in the midnight
The woods are still and dry
Timeless and unworldly now
As if poised for ever

Bails of hay are stacked and
Their scent rises slowly
Young men and women find
Themselves so unclothed

What pattern do they create
In their careless loving
Upon the powdery earth and
Its ancient clinging dust

In the fullness of their passion
The sky above flashing lightly
What impulse of the universe
Is secured in what they hold

11 - 27

THE beauty of a new young moon
Slim candid and so innocent
Like knowledge without belief
Feckless and yet compelling

Tawny bronze and shining
Are the small dry apples
Evening shadows now incline
Long sensuous and satisfied

Sensing a sudden cool air
Trees change their clothing
Prepare to undress quietly
Exposing their limbs

Do you remember that land
Where cyclamen and poppies
Would appear now as the sea
Along the coast became cold

If immortality is the knowing
That we do not exist
Then mariners who set out
Voyaging toward truth -

Approach that strange shore
Within a human heart
Where rays of light are greater
Than the sun of any life

Paths where we once walked
Sometimes sleeping in the groves
Where cicadas proclaimed noon
And dust was perfectly still

The art of voyaging becomes
Our genius for grief
Knowing what was given as
Undying - without amnesty

The nakedness of young life
And easiness of pleasure
Immutable is the bride
Within these falling hours

We pass through those flames
Purified of our own poor fire
A few embers remain
Hidden among the rocks

Those loves which failed
Which can never be retrieved
Nor resharpened with a spark
Nor invisible knife -

We cannot endure a life
Of infidelity where speech
Has no tense and faith
Is stripped of humility

How quickly the sun goes
So fast is human blood
We keep nothing in our arms
Except what time incurs

Worthless yet compelling
Is the need for sweet fruit
The destiny of affection
Or lucid universe revealed

I I – 2 8

THE beauty of lakes
In their solitude
Covered in shadow
Where kingfishers love

The beauty of rivers
Strong and motive
Whose current is home
When ships return

The beauty of mariners
Who know these things
Unspeakable coasts
Terrain they have touched

Beauty of leaves
Making masts and spars
Ribbed decks of boats
Which journey at sea

How life is displaced
By a bevelled wind
As it draws on a sail
Taking vessels away

True lovers who
Simply know all this
To navigate
Old skies and stars

Black sinuous shoals
Mirror the flashing
Of dry naked clouds
In a vacant sphere

Where years circle
As cranes now depart
Swallows humming-birds
Even small falcons

Some visit the luminous
Invisible isles
Others tread darkness
So compulsively

This autonomous life
As trees become boats
Or young men and women
Grow silent in time

On impossible paths
Unbetrayed they
Struggle with death
Ordeals to be free

Enjoined by sorrow
To suffer apart
Where courage inwardly
Happily bounds

A voice from the sea
Is calling them home
Ingenuous light
With its cargo of dust

Those who love
The beauty of water
Are never alone
Or among the stars lost

11 – 29

THE suffering of light is not shadowy
But consciousness of moral dark
Obsidian and elliptical
Yet profound in its dignity
Becoming everything on earth
Possible to apprehension
Even life that gleams beyond the sun

We fail to comprehend the beautiful
In auburn-crimson autumn's slow
Fruition that transforms us from
The fertile and creative
To that black instant before renewal
When we briefly realise how true
Were all the errors and illusion

What rings can marry us to life
In this fugitive death of the year
What circles of conception
Shall bring us to that presence
Of beautifully moving truth
What courage drives a narrow river
Toward a cold grey infinite sea

How wonderful is grief itself
Marking us with empty love
For suffering - light is universal
Completely without pause or rest
We ourselves are those slim shadows
Sheltering beneath obscure trees
As the sun goes to its west

for Pia Maybury-Lewis

11-30

BEHOLD that man that one
Of implacable finesse
Who standing in the wind
In cold stiletto rain
Smiles at our distress

That woman who despite
All the gathering darkness
Where dead leaves are swept
Into the same old river
Only smiles at our enigma

Behold the infant boy or girl
Who dancing barefoot shouts
For the pleasure of a song
Words that have no meaning
Laughing at each minute -

The seconds and the instants
That are tissue and blood
Fluid substance and thread
Of all our unnumbered days
Consumed and justly diminished

Behold how we renew
Naked and mysterious now
For slowness is always beautiful
As the true sun of life
Constantly returns

Behold the fresh devotion
The lover and the young kind
Every small animated being
Creatures who join impassioned
To realise one moment's joy

We struggle in the vineyard
Among a thousand fallen leaves
To acquire one pure wet taste
Where the world is not deceived
And there is just reception

Snow now unifies the earth
Within a singular perfection
As lovers in their first sweetness
Witness the nerves revealed -
There is nothing like that

Large dark birds are waiting
Blue and rouge in the trees
Stepping quietly through the grass
They stare at us in silence
Waiting for our breath to pause

For this is all we know
The seed in the grain and
The water in the sky falling
Wind passing across our face
As the universe says repeatedly
Behold the only promise

I I – 3 1

UNDER thin metal oak leaves
Vibrating in frozen west wind
Deer and owls are collecting
Foxes come to sniff at bones
Under a pink and apricot dawn

A hawk strips a poor meal
A rabbit limps for want of grass
Crows are silenced by the cold
Cross a bare cerulean sky
Above the mineral oak leaves

Whose the grey bones the hair
Whose the slow starvation
Did anyone desire that body once
When it was gold and heated

I I – 3 2

THE first thin snow silences
A world with its evening
Small birds grow quiet as
Shadows seep to the earth

A colourless sky descends
With slow circular mystery
As cold watery vapour
Gathers about points of life

Unspeakably lone and separate
We await an ideal birth
A young and avid new light
With all goodness of kind

In their nakedness the trees
Move slightly in desperation
Coldness enters into stone
The river struggles with darkness

Pheasant woodcock and quail
Eyes closed with hunger
Hide carefully amid the stubble
Fox and rabbit halt and wait

Fields remain untouched now
Deer tread vigilant in search
Of rare grass and sustaining moss
To sleep among damp reeds

We pause in our oblivion
Surrendering to solitude
Where milky radiance hovers
Urging us toward a fire

If consciousness is apart
From this sensible world
That experience is our truth
Origin of living amity

What ancient feet now walk
On raw granite hills
What features of the universe
Oversee our dubiety -

Ribbons of experience and
Fabric of all sensation
A nucleus of certain union
Joining creatures in their rest

This one true cell in which
We first become aware
Like an undefended child
Staring at an icy world

The frail snow censors
Human ignition and suffering
As shadows justly promise
Intimacy and affection

11–33

INITIATIVE of light and birds
Passing through a gateway
Hills draw ancient darkness
Where fidelity vibrates

We are wreathed in coldness
Enclosed by damp earth
The cadence of lovers
Is hidden among leaves

When you love do not
Let it fly from your hands
Regardless of misery
Or its cause of despair

Like the keel of a boat
Or an autumn plough
Copper nails rusting and
Oars so abandoned -

This boat has wings and
Its torn crimson hull
Has two black eyes
That are always famished

If you love then all
The world is observed
However solitary
Your excluded hours

If you love you receive
One just gift of vision
To be always a witness
Of what no one knows

Through mineral gates
Our life shall depart
Stripped of lightness
As if shot from a bow

Like the mystery of music
Yet no anthem is heard
An incendiary predator
Who calls out in time

As boats have their vision
Pursue lonely courses
Without oblivion
Is this human archery

Despite our removal
Grainy dust of years
What you love becomes
More perfect than kind

Hovering in silence
And lightly inspected
We are simply weighed
As we pass like birds

You are the lover and
No one is apart
For loving has joined you
Outside of this world

If the aim is life
And the end is true
There is no death
Given your promise

I I – 3 4

I AM silenced by your beauty
Fluent light of your eyes
Stainless immoveable and lovely
Is your unbreakable desire

The misery that you inspired
And resentment cultivated
All these like summer rain
Could not overwhelm the fountain

In love with the unbetrothed
You turned into stone
And thinking of your freedom
You only became impulsive

Now you age beyond life
And at evening recall
So much reckless dalliance
Nothing can make you smile

Yet your beauty makes me quiet
There is water in your laughter
Even the garments you wear
Still imply your loveliness

What is to be said at last
There are flaws in our vision
Should slaves become impassioned
By what they never possess

I I – 3 5

I THOUGHT my grief would never end
That my solitude would fill the world
And I would die of weeping
That no one on earth would know

Like wild grass that falls and dies
Without the warmth of summer rain
So I thought my time was finished
When you went away this morning

Love can travel a thousand miles
In less than one second
And when we die all that remains
Is life – that is what they say

In the engine-room of the heart
There always is a sound of beating
Even if there is no wind
Sails move back and forth

Since your departure I
Am subtracted by futility
There remains no happiness
In any second any more

So I have lightly climbed
This invisible iron stair
For so many years alone
Without companion voice

This solitary grey ascent
Where even swallows and hawks
Have departed from these skies
Of quickly changing colour

The wind runs round about
Circling spherical days
What is there now to see
And - must we still arise

Without you I am vacant
Dry motionless and untouched
Without your wild sea-mood of blood
This world becomes so speechless

11 – 36

EARLY morning like a shepherd
Through dense grey light
Going by fields and rivers
Protecting immortality from time

Where we wait for the wind
In a silent trickling air
As cold thin arid rain
Drives away human radiance

If the mystery of suffering
Is this perfect challenge
The secrecy of courage
Becomes our call or demand

It is so dark and the sun
Just touches our blood
Taking us from life toward
That long moral arch

Where the sun steps forward
Barefoot onto wet grass
Like friendship – the day
Revives us with its eyes

So what was all that loving
Such tense intoxication
Were those companions truly
Patient in their honesty

When the armour of speech
Shone like refracted fire
And the visor of affection
Covered our weak parts

Was there an ardent cause
Blue moment when a cry
Emptied the world of solitude
In that first early morning

Early morning as the night
And its darkness decease
When the origin of our kind
And fragrance is hidden

What might we conceive
As we fall asleep at last
What image like a hawk
Passes before our vision

Early morning as we stare
At friends who approach
Saluting from the shadow
Calling us to join their pace -

Upon a small white boat
That stills its sails a moment
Waiting for us to board
To set off one more time

On a fertile glittering sea
Without sky or horizon
Translucent and untouchable
In its unspeakable ways

That traceless new voyage
Where insensible at last
Our conscious body is
Weightless and without pain

I I – 3 7

BRING some water it is time
To drink to swear our end
Run the boat towards the edge
Now we must go home

Fetch white oars from racks
Embrace old friends and take
The hard-wood tiller from
Above the hearth - bring grain
For the advancing future

Soon ice will sheathe our blades
Then thirst will make us dumb
Wounds will refuse to join
Lips be sore and hardened
Now we have said everything

Leave behind the torn charts
We know the sun's routine
We have our own metaphors
We breathe - a laughless sea
The shell of night awaits

White canvas covers the hull
Stiff upon frames and ribs
A lack of gravity keeps us
From falling onto rocks
For we have nothing to lose

Bring water let us drink
Unclothed and undisguised
We only wear a visor now
Our souls are made of water
Lift the hull toward the edge

When the sun a milky spot
In the sky and we unseen
Stripped of all but memory
Then we truly live - stayed
By lucid friendship

Ospreys will follow diving
Into our wake for fish
Petrels shall build their nest
In foam left by our stem
Dolphins bring us to sleep

The glare of a true sun
Will cleanse our icy purpose
Saline green of swell will teach
Us to repeat - initial words
We once learned to say

We are the first ship and
Sea-deities will amaze to see
Us crossing above - they
Who thought they were alone
Potent undenied till now

Sea-weed sea-gull gleaming
Sand-bank flats where rivers
Fuse their current in the draw
And withdrawal of salt tide
Low stony isles of pine forest

A few rough spars beached
Will be all that ever remains
To sing of us and tell
How we vanished from life
Disappeared from a world

Printed by dustless forms
Our songs are whiter than
Marble or breaking wave
Stronger than brass or iron
Letters pressed in granite base

Neither rain nor rust nor
Death's liberty nor melting
Fire can touch them now
We have gone home where
None but friendship counts

Thinking we never end
Between houses we left
And islands recalled there
Is only pretence of dignity
Trials of kindness - say

Like a bottle of water
Dropped into an ocean
Sinking before it breaks
Like a pebble of salt
Dissolved in the sea
Fusing in cold waves

In our adventures
We are consumed
Vanish into the rest
As glass shatters and
Water mixes with ocean
We become all that we were

I I – 3 8

WHAT is the grain of these days
What vessel can we build
And store its hold for years
Of long and solitary voyage

So build yourself a firm ship
That shall never founder
Made of wind and trees and iron
For every course of happiness

Make a compass out of love
A hull bound with affection
Giving more than it receives
To all the passing waves

May the fragrance of the ocean
Archery of a starry heaven
Drive the ship through all its years
Until we forget our name

May your companions be like birds
With their secret midnight music
And may all the shadowy fish
Keep your course away from rocks

Place hard stones upon your keel
To remind you of the misery
That you put aside when leaving
Port and all that old grief

For that will bring you gravity
Shall keep your boat upright
Despite sharp gales that torment
When no breeze moves your heart

Then one day when that white isle
Appears to be before your eyes
As anchors fall and sails collapse
And you are free of ordeal

On that shore of happiness
There is no print upon the sand
There is no one and no body
Where you lie down and rest

11-39

THERE are two cities on earth
Divided by time and kindness
And at the centre of their field
Is a king who sits in silence

About him move the reapers
Drawing in the living grain
Goodness or the void deceit
That human life advances

On the edges of this world
Just beyond the known blue rim
Are mortal doubt and anxiety
Glittering with so much disbelief

In one city there is despair
Meaningless desolation
Where sickles of severe abuse
Cut and harvest emptiness

Sometimes moral predators
Destroy us in the night
When ambushed by cruelty
We are wrecked by extreme contempt

In another city there is judgement
Where a palpable soul is weighed
And the words our tongues exchange
Are assessed for generosity

Beyond the urban walls there is
A worn green altar on a plain
Where smoke is offered to the sky
And blood poured on the stones

There are the unwritten stars
Calculating every hour
Few who walk this level world
Observe their silence and precision

There are brides grooms and lovers
Where the youthful go apart
To meet indelibly and completely
Offering all they might possess

There are songs of the universe
That recall for us a truth
Words forsaken in our effort
When we only pursue ourselves

There are small lakes and rivers
Running down toward a coast
And on the hills are quick hawks
Who play upon a thin grey wind

There are vineyards and groves
And orchards where boys and girls
Laugh among the grassy shadow
Lightly clothed with future promise

Just like a dancing floor all this
Was prepared without a single wound
Perfectly beautiful and still
Where years are made immobile

Although we see the movement
Are impelled by human currency
Yet nothing happens or can change
In the eyes of this ardent king

for Gregory Nagy

III - 1

A STRETCH of grass and a stone
Clouds above and trees about
You beside me in the light
As we waken to the world

The rhythm of your bones
Your eyebrows that tell all
Sweetness of your skin and
The irreverence you play

When dragonflies were born
A thousand years ago
To live and die in minutes
Yet essential to the world -

Or like planets that arise
In the crimson hour before dawn
Where life is not distinguished
As it appears and disappears -

We hold those moments in a field
Surrounded by the speechless stones
Where a few fractions of intimacy
Reveal all the universe

Our stillness and its quietness
As small insects drift the air
Expose to us the covenant
That makes life possible on earth

Trees birds shadows dust
One instant holds all of time
All experience and all knowledge
Like your beauty in my hands -

All the promises we adored
Like the elegance of old trees
Or treasured vows received
From long ago affirmed

Transitory enchanted moments
That we could never refrain
Only the false made us suffer
When love was the bread we broke

There are many parts of speech
Most of them unknown
Sometimes we hear those words
That no one else can tell

Awareness is not consciousness
You have touched me so often
Yet you never knew the heart
That moved beneath your hand

Then sea-blue woman - you
Who divided fire from water
You took our grief and buried
All of time beneath stones

If only we had been true
We might have foregone suffering
For beside those chilling waves
We were apart from ourselves

The autumn realm deepens now
To darken life as leaves fall
Radiant transcendental evening
Restores low red shadow

As the sacred geese move south
Quivering and yet so doubtless
We who walk upon the grass
Are there simply to observe

If unconditional love is all
That we might ever achieve
Without anticipation or affection
Experience of benevolence -

Then everything becomes removed
And the most we might accomplish
Is to offer a most perfect bond
Admiring what we do not know

To listen is to honour
To remain silent at offence
Never to criticise despair
Nor the anger of ignorance

For only in the arms of kind
Where men and women rest
Might they embrace the universe
Just as the world rotates

We are part of a single passion
Bearing within us potential life
So there is no decease only
One rare second of perfection

I I I – 2

THE one syllabled god who walks
Impartial in all creatures
Unaverted who has no proof
Whose mastery is in splendour

Created for sensible eyes
A grey falcon out of softness
Light and small muscles
Like steel and a knife for a beak

The bird knew the air - was kin
To the sun and all its points
Lived high among rocks
Fed on red flesh and cold water

In flames it entered light
Loving the glare of the sky
An impulse purely heat as
The undiminished food of time

Fearless and intangible
Folded throughout space
The bird assumed volition
Equal to the desire of play

Deified - when it died
It turned to coppery fire
A missile of invulnerable kind
Passing between lovers

Yet all passion vanishes
Adhesive to the human heart
When no longer prey a soul
Becomes dustless and undying

This courage of sublunary life
It also comes and goes
Moves with invisible darkness
Forms colours and flares

Now the wind runs her hand
Throughout stiff trees
Searching for a river or lake
Where to sleep alone

Then from pure cerulean
To clear turquoise water
Dawn's matrix continually
Opens her thin arms

Our age with all its shadows
And such a love of youth
Is incapable of resisting
This fire being so eternal

Harvested and threshed
In circles made of old light
Our mortal grain is weighed
And our small truth separated

The sand of all our worth
Without weight or any colour
Is stored away in time
Just like our bones are buried

From courage virtue and defeat
Comes our nameless goodness
In that mastery we are sealed
Made distinct from air

So in our acts of love
What we might achieve
Is a forgiveness of those
Without universal life

The art of life is not enduring
Is not detached from any way
The slight vision we achieve
Is a just truth of solitude

That is our sole act of liberty
That untimed conception when
The universe becomes exposed
Its body turning into light

The only perfect sphere is
Not the sun nor time
But what appears when we close
Our eyes and there is no sound

I I I - 3

THE quiet mind is ardent
Conceived of native light
Among shadows and the stones
Upon the grass at evening

Or a star alone in its suspense
Like grain at conception
Whose beauty is the destiny
Of its own ambition

Above a resounding sea
Swans and geese are conveyed
Their inward vision poised upon
What no human sight perceives

The sea retreats in time
Advancing durable and circular
Drawn by sullen lunar fire
Without bitterness or monotony

Now the defective season
Closes both her chilling eyes
There is no pattern nor imprint
No mirror to revive us

Now summer like a queen
In venous-coloured midnight
With her final yellow sparks
Retires toward the underworld

Our desire for perpetuation
Exceeds all human shadow
Beyond the clouds always
The sun is shining deeply

That bed where all summer
You and I lay on the grass
No one knows what happened
There nor of that mystery

For briefly we then became
Changeless and supernal
As beneath an indifferent sky
We fled the impermanent

If there is no fidelity in life
And only passing amity
The cold spray of timeliness
Might resolve earthly remorse

Like the swallows and starlings
Rising from our limbs to fly
So the fiction of our making
Became a mastery of love

Then freed we do not return
To any natural place or form
Despite the beauty and serenity
Of these transcendent days

Life travels with such haste
And we apprehend so little
Even lovers soon forget
What they gathered embracing

If we receive our solitude
Within another's hold
Noosed by a heart a heart
Might dissemble its unbecoming

If life is just a mirror here
And no one is truly present
We replicate another world
Woven upon gorgeous fabric

Is there any flawless ring
That we might put on and wear
To marry us and join us
In the experience of promise

Let us make the infinite tangible
Without any hesitation
The inspection of a long night
Strips us of imperfection

So love more than you can
Laugh most at humiliation
For losing is a generous gift
Circling our way

III - 4

LIKE a far-off distant beating
As if of engines out at sea
Where vessels pass beyond horizon
Unseen except for their sounding

Or like the swell of current
Tidal motion of the blood
Or the currency of stars as
We wander and we turn

Be with us now in this time
When ice first films the lake
When the river slows and darkens
And days become like night

Relieve our body of its weight
Of all temper and of change
So the dense universe appears
Before us face to face

In the still heart of stone
There you are a mineral wave
A slow tuning of earth's pulse
A sound or distant tremor

The rocks murmur and the trees
In an undertone of wind
As lovers tell their affection
In the most profound hours

Naked limbs now touch heaven
Winter light is thin as bone
So you reform your love
Exposing your certain outline

For only through bare justice
Does a threshold appear in time
As we take small tacit steps
And touch the hand of beauty

For you are unborn and
Have seen a thousand years
Made of carbon and of stone
Aware of all that moves on earth

The archery of your vision
Whose unearthly fire once fell
In love beneath the moon
And adored the darting sunlight -

Like gold leaf so fragile
Easily displaced by light or air
You still surround those who
Are willing to be alone

The true light in your eyes
Then takes us to where
A true sky and true stars
Sign themselves upon our bodies

For life always re-appears
Honesty cannot be broken
If only one voice sings to us
Making us truly sonorous

Like the moral and ingenious
Silence of the kind river
As it recedes in tawny dusk
Anointing us with cold rites

I I I – 5

THE beauty of imperfection
Is all that we might hold
In life time days or words
As suddenly light becomes quiet

The squares are deserted now
The river empty of boats
No one works the ridged fields
No one knows why we are waiting

This vernal time of magnolia
Of hyacinth and crocus
Of a young new moon in
A blue evening of unseen birds

For only birds know our truth
As they travel across seasons
Like raptors who apprehend
All our moral indecision

If love is not to be completed
There is only one sure action
To give more than we receive
So nothing else exists

As we walk the dry pavement
Moving among uncut stones
The hours fall constantly
Heat and shade define our heart

Then when we surrender
Submit to what we do not know
That is the one passion
Which conveys us on in time

Only in slowness do we appear
Candid and strangely careless
Perceiving all we cannot become
For there is never any pausing

This slight partition of the stars
Which exists within our eyes
We might never touch their body
Yet we are made amorous

As if a groom before a bride
In the suddenness of passion
When humility makes us vulnerable
As the season is disclosed

For woman's love for man
And man's love of woman
Are random not symmetrical
Profoundly out of time

If unfulfilled love is trapped
Made absent from experience
What mystery destroys love
Tears apart our substance

In the falling down of affection
In solitude we must admit
What can never be reversed
When courage becomes timely

No hammer of any wisdom
Nor flame of stainless vision
Can remove the verve from this
Fluency and fury of light

For a while we only rest
Among stones beneath the trees
Sheltering in light and shade
As if death was not perfect

So long endures patience
Whirlpools of infinite sadness
Yet our animating principle
Remains infallible and true

We are bathers in a stream
Particles of embodied ardour
Unaware and nude standing
In so many thousand years

We enter upon an infinite sea
Touch hands as we swim
Submerge and leave no trace
Upon the soft grey water

III-6

ON this threshing floor of days
As we sing to the evening river
Covered in leaves small skins of life
An alizarin sky craves its moment

The headlong passion of these days
Light-footed like a dancer
Moves sanguine until fatal night
Takes off our resistance

Soon no one will walk
Where we are going now
Down these burnt paths and
Printless tracks of an old hillside

Lost to an obedient future
Light gathers without presence
At dawn the limbs of morning
Are both motive and disturbing

Those who have gone have time
To watch us as we wind
Upon this circling ground
Treading more straw than grain

For human sensibility is always
Searching for its symmetry
Love that makes blood flow
To multiply a living heart

Spring amounts in light and warmth
As trees begin to run with life
Sweet fluid drips and small birds
Return and search for new branches

The virtuous eyebrows of these days
Whose austerity like a fuse
Burns away our poor livelihood
Aloof and quick with compulsion -

So human spirit flies in time
Revives having forgotten
An immaterial world where
Kindness was the only force

From breath to breath we go
We speak and kiss or drink
Drawing on the air of love
Making us impassioned

What to say when deceasing
If nothing ever changed
In so much singing of desire
A setting out of our admission

If the aim of vision has no way
No gorgeous cloth nor show
Just an unmoved inward temper
Where admiration is perfected -

That is our only rapture
Which can never be exchanged
Nor can it ever be exposed
Beyond a shining act of promise

So beauty that is transient
Incapable of being held
Leads us to the unearthly
Where we are not dispossessed

In happiness is no duration
We are stripped of likely suffering
Then apprehend how we are seen
And conceived without aim

Just as grass grows from water
With gifts from a guiding sun
Dust is raised by movement
Nothing is still except love

I I I - 7

THE running of a human soul
From rain to lake to river
Toward the slow glossy sea
Where the universe is lucid

All our freezing now surrenders
As showers cross the land
Spears of coldness fall down
Before the eyes of warm spring

Recall and anticipation
Find their equilibrium
As we reform our love
Without grains of remorse

It is not the shining hour
Nor the perfect glance
But the experience of balance
That appears so attractive

A dry vernal wind blows
Drawing on our wonder
Causing us to simply crave
Turn away from darkness

To end the fearful misery
Of late winter when
No croci ever breaks upon
A hard frigid earth

Sacred birds are flying
Laughter visits in a field
Boats convey new currency
On the water's soft green flood

The goodness of this single day
Advancing and inherent
Eradicating natural doubt
Annihilating so much grief

There is only one occasion
On this round curving world
From which all moral life
Radiates without source

The message of the sunlight
Tells of that destiny
A subtle landscape where
Kindness might rest

For beauty always returns
To stand before us and
The sanctity of the animate
Is how we are affirmed

Now we are undisguised
Deficient of all emptiness
Young heroes walk apart
In their brightness of vision

We remember and we hope
So imperfect love
Might justly happen once
Giving more than is received

Then all our decaying
The weakness and disuse
Will be at last forsaken
Those trials we made in time

How it was we attempted
To make the beautiful apparent
To restore the lightly human
To its true inheritance

The blood of this goodness
Weightless and transparent
Runs out onto cool air
All of life is so appeased

I I I - 8

KINGS stand in the sunlight
Lions are at their prayer
Hawks touch the air for pleasure
As trees now prepare for love

Loving-kind or human tyranny
Going through untimely days
Listen to the wind tonight
Like a spirit far from home

These moveable days when
Grain keeps to its sheath
Before the dry fragile leaflet
Begins to soften and unfold

Speech vibrates with hidden warmth
In the throats of young birds
New songs are declaimed
And shadows stretch at length

In our election and pursuit
There is no betrayal
For in solitude we admit
What can never be reversed

The doubling of emotion now
When the vernal runs and moves
As unseen to human eyes
The amorous cries out for time

Now the white dogwoods
With their queenly pause
Hover in a lucid air
Disregarding rainfall

There among changeless stones
So many lives are at rest
In sleep oblivion and yet
With perfect vision in their eyes

A golden disc now covers
The world and obscures
The personification of a star
Paradise without shadow

Under a glittering interleaving
Sweetness of white pear blossom
An exaltation of minutes
Holds our transparency close

For the perfect lacks all gravity
Being lucid and unsigned
Where eyes never close and
No breath finds suspense

Where triumphant light exposes
A quiet heart that instils us
Its genius making us benign
Always springing to the air –

The black and white of time
Sunlight and its circling
Like a river made of shadow
Flowing deep into the earth

Who then perceives a perfect
Love in that incessant night
Uninhabited by human-kind
Occupied only by the quiet

In true love is no duration
Breath has no cadence
We see throughout the darkness
That moves upon a human form

Kings and queens of the universe
Silently admire these days
The flourishing and dancing
Of gentle benevolence

I I I - 9

IN the night a hawk sleeps
Unaware of any lightness
Except for the perpetual fire
That motivates its passion

The dragon-fly or swallow
The humming-bird or falcon
Each migrates through days of time
Passing from pretext into clouds

This universe is made of night
Of coldness without rain
There are no shadows moving
Among those silent minerals

The beauty of the human body
Always crescent never deficient
Like human contemplation that
Translates us with new vision

Abounding rainfall in the night
Like courage – requires no audience
Only certainty brings us life
Throughout our changeless hours

There is no fragrance in the night
No warmth which to adore
Darkness has no offspring
And is itself its own circle

The ambitious lovers who
Waken together on a lake shore
One spring dawn as swallows
Descend to earth and new light

All night their rare affection
Among the senseless shadows
Remains untouched by time
For so fulfilled they are

Inflexible and justly weightless
Transparent with all strength
The pattern of the universe
Rests within their hands

Upon their lips and eyes
In their hair and on their limbs
The meeting of all moments
Is completely re-enacted

Such perfect amity cannot decay
Nor lose possession of its ways
For mutually they never fail
Their passion does not go apart

By a simple act of human flight
They are in faith with the wind
Being imprinted by the stars
As they cross a sightless land

For the union of all things
Even what we cannot say
Is imperative and indelible
Impelling every given gesture

The rainfall offers us its hands
A possibility of human love
Where water is inspired to run
And a cry of joy is heard

III–10

THE most beautiful day on earth
Hovers and then passes
Among light-hearted trees
As dragon-flies pause on the lake

Pied beauty of the summer
Whose mask of light and dark
Hangs and shines above us now
Aware of only itself

There is a diamond in the air
Shining deep within our hearts
And like an eagle or heron
It descends to meet our eye

This is the ring that lovers wear
Made of light and transparent stone
That weightless cannot be destroyed
Nor can it be exchanged

Like a shallow dish of spotless water
That might never be withheld
Or those perfect figures who approach
In suspense above our solitude

This ring joins us in the world
Away from living human hours
And when we drink of this love
Suffering is stripped and falls

There is nothing else on earth
No vessel moving through the days
For once we accept this moment
There is no possible rest

A music given to our hands
The water in our blood
The choice to continue loving
When sorrow has no use

Being so impressed by
This slight grey elusive nucleus
Of humility and patience
Austere and impermanent -

Like a beautiful young leopard
Summer crept upon us
Crouching low and observant
Lost in a pattern of shade

Or like a curious lion moving
Lightly through dry grass
Summer stalked the solemn fields
Looking for its bloody prey

The evening voice of swallows
Is a small threading of sound
Deer rest in cold shadow
And falcons remain still

For now the perfect lovers
Who lie on the harvested dust
Their touch halts and pauses
And their slowness is forever

For here there is no future
We cross a bridge from the past
Gifts of time in open hands
Are offered to an invisible fire

III – 11

A CARMINE redness of new dawn
Advances toward all eyes
Light that moves us in its arms
To light that we cannot say

Young swallows in midsummer
On dry warm evening air
Light touching on the underside
Of their quick sharp wings

They appear in the twilight
Above rivers and green lakes
To glide above prolific trees
Subtly vivid and communal

A perfect work of art they are
Certain like the rain at night
That vivifies a sleeping world
Arousing every love of kind

Small golden blades of life
Made of wind and distance
Created of a thousand miles
Flashing through millennia

Their love is immediate
Untroubled by compulsion
Without anticipation or
Any foresight of grief

Consilient genius of truth
As their flight fits the air
Weightless and so buoyant
They easily migrate in time

Both past and the future
Stay within their vision
As they travel and return like
Threads weaving consciousness

Midsummer when decease
Begins to make its way
The sun moves behind trees
And thin shadows descend

There is a hidden ring in this
Quiet shuttering of blue air
Fitting us profoundly and
Formed of blood and trivial bone

The swallows briefly entertain
Each other with their rites
Then having given to the earth
Transparent life they depart

A perfect universal beauty
With no morality of darkness
As they reach and touch the hand
That fashioned them completely

I I I – 1 2

IF our masterpiece is universal
Delivers us our knowing
To follow us in time and
Captivate with pattern -

Now our light hovers
Like dust above dry fields
On haying and the gathering
Of deer and foals in shadow

We are that darkness where
Awareness is observing
So many small birds panting
Beneath noon's humidity

Now the wheat is singing
As summer loses its head
Victorious swallows simply
Skim a calm warm lake

These days are executioners
Destroying our untruth
Whose blades remove all
Consciousness of disaffection

There is no duration now
A glass of water is consumed
Just as we are poured out
And life becomes invisible

You became my masterpiece
Made more than ephemeral
By perfecting and refining
All aspects of your worldliness

We cannot discard hunger
Nor that thirst for love
And yet in days forgotten
We surrendered every breath

As tidal streams and rivers
Merge with cold green sea
You are my beautiful island
Where lightness never ceases

So vision now advances
To unknown empty fields
On forests hills and coasts
With a mastery we once pursued

I I I – 1 3

IN this great water - river of swans
We are interred and there is no grief
For the survival of loving always
Exceeds our futility of effect

From a gentle hill of stones
We look down upon
That dark and so recurving
Sinuous procession of water

This river of love on which
We stare as the sunlight
Vanishes from earth and sky
And coldness covers our feet

Fish birds small creatures
High reed and dry grasses
Tall willows that profoundly drink
Of mercurial fresh green current

This is the river of affection
Of friendship and all motive
How we are now impelled and
Conducted through time

That is the place where we go
Where the sun is always rising
Where quiet deer and fox patrol
And owl and hawk are watching

There foals stand in the shadows
The dyed sea is awaiting
And we are not unnoticed
When love calls from a distance

There no one sleeps nor deceases
Children never age nor fall
Where marriages and wedding feasts
Continue without terminus

Then human speech becomes
A just work of perfection
Where words remain changeless
On the tongues of men and women

Once I held you in my arms
In a small room above that shore
Where ships arrived and cargoes
Transferred from destinations

Despite the many shifts of time
We willingly revive our thirst
Each day renew the passion
Of optimism - love of kindness

Step by step be with me now
Let us move beyond those hours
Going further than life concedes
Toward that place we only know

My many mooded river
Both black and so profound
Green lover of floe and
Quiet irregular mist -

Creator and remaker
Going beyond the years
You fill our hearts with admiration
Drawn from the universe

Even during darkness you
Continue running through the land
Privately conveying us
Toward a goodness unheard

Grey slow and ambivalent
Descended from a brazen sky
You bring to us a flood
Of cyanine and crimson waves

One day the laughing swallows
Shall glide above your way
As from lake to sea you flow
Taking us by the hand

Genius of all blood and
Bride of sailing vessels
Bearing in your heart a ring
Crowning us with happiness

Familiar of every gateway
Old worn cities of this world
Marriages and obsequies
That make life so true

Messenger of men and women
You join them at night
Sleeping upon the stones
Where the future is conceived

III-14

THE choirs that compose our lives
Birds cicadas wind rainfall
Someone calling out our name
When there is no one present

So we lightly part the air
With words or with footsteps
A vast immortal order we
Do not observe yet inhabit

How simply the supernatural
Exceeds the merely human
Yet almost all of life is
Lost from any possible recall

Those who are heartbroken
Who only long for sleep
Still crave for that one second
That inner hold of recognition

Time races past them yet
They apprehend so little
Accomplish even less in
Thoughtful passages and ways

What unchanging work of art
Just like a perfect heartbeat
Might - radiant and ephemeral
Restore them to amity

What was it we received
In so much passion and pursuit
What moved within our eyes as
Now the last breath advances

Summer-winter go beyond us
Trees and birds are revived
Grasses incline their hair
The wind is filtered by rain

So let us listen for that sound
Inaudible and unspoken
Whose material perfection
Is candid and anonymous

For no gesture of affection
Might resolve the grief of silence
That perpetual solitude
Hidden in the heart of kind

I I I – 1 5

A PATHLESS barefoot sea where
Lights of fisher boats glow in space
Where at night sea-broken stones
Put a hand through the water

Where the women are always waiting
Listening to the sound of waves
The same long old monody
Telling of beauty and distance -

The truth of quiet sorrow
A tireless unclothed song of time
Where destiny and pathos remain
To be forever unsaid

In a mild topaz-crimson light
Uprising from speechless water
A small grey empty moon
Lay supine on the endless current

With the whiteness of a shell or
Softness of a young hawk
Or bitterness of new salt
Freshly taken from the shore -

The loneliness of human effort
Threshed and winnowed by
So many strongly driven years
Footprints without measure

Some of us fell in love and
Found kindness when we married
In those silvery shining groves
Juvenile and responsive

Yet to see a tree from one side
Then to see it from the other
And to continue the journey –
That is our only fidelity

Gentle consonants of the heart
Vowels of our breathing where
Every moral word becomes
In time thoroughly unique

Mountains turn to mineral dust
Motionless and darkened
Birdless and uninhabited
Light runs away forever

We waited and pretended
In the sparse evening hours
For radiant solitude to exalt us
Each day being more honest

In our fragility we made haste
Yet the sea always outpaced us
Time removed us from that light
Becoming so transparent

for L.H.

III-16

WHAT is possible is ordained
Like the nuance in your eyes
Or light symmetry when we
Walk together before night

It is difficult to pretend
That we do not exist
For that implies generosity
An apprehension of truth

Yet we cannot endure a life
Of infidelity where hours
Have no heart and days
Are stripped of humility

No matter what endures
There is always a pattern in
Time and its partition
If we do not fear

Restless at evening as
We slowly return from ourselves
The pleasure of a closed room
Away from human confinement -

Unbetrothed and unbetrayed
As lovers of spring who
Are perfectly tense in our play
Upon the music of passion

So it is that time discloses
As it prowls and devours
And we miss the light
Only praising the moment

We did not know of loneliness
Nor the cruelty of solitude
Imperative and yielding we
Were only aware of nature's design

Years later we shall recall
The completion of this time
How we were so impelled
Yet oblivious of our treasure

Restless at the end of life
We reclaim that upstairs room
How it was to fall asleep
Exhausted by happiness

When the first snow arrives
Descending onto the black river
Upon hard dry grasses
Sharp stems of fallen grain -

Swallows will have departed
With their small quick breath
As heron geese and hawks
Retreat from cold sunless day

As we pass through those gates
Pretending to be life itself
As a deer becomes a tree
And then simply vanishes -

A heart that does not move
Cannot love and so loving
Everything is the greatest
Of all acts of compassion

Having drunk away our thirst
We turn back to the light
Forget the truth which we held
All that was only beautiful -

As a dove might murmur or
A nightingale can sing
A lark vanish into sound
Yet the entirety of vision stays

III - 17

WE hear slow engines beating
Hum of motors in the night
As unseen vessels silently
Approach where we embark

Taking us toward islands
Beautiful remote and unknown
Where we might walk the hills
Sleep on the shores in love

There is no morality to despair
No disillusion when we know
Only white birds in the trees
And nuptial meals prepared

So we struggled with futility
Remorse contempt and cruelty
That was our only work
Freeing us from compulsion

That bloody filthy fire where
Awareness was conceived
Beside a hearth of stone
When flames inscribed the night

There is difficulty in being
Good kind or careless
When action speech and thought
Avoid human decency -

So much fatality and
So little to be accomplished
In parades and memorials for
A vast emptiness of days

For earthly ingenuity
Cannot exceed the passages
That swallows apprehend
Nor the plan of a weaver-bird -

Or in the vision of a hawk
In the progress of coyotes
Or a red fox as it travels land
Wandering for millennia

Only human artistry
With the supernature of its work -
One rare golden masterpiece
Might transform our weak lives

For the genius of vital truth
Only fits the eyes of those
Unaware of themselves
Or of their own reflection

Regardless of where we are
Experience shall deliver all -
A sound of ships beyond horizon
Takes us from a pitiless world

III-18

THERE is a mirror in the world
Where we might view our lives
Called solitude when we
Become absent from ourselves

In that city of light there is
No one and in the city
Of love there is no body
No sign of any kind

For all occurs at once
We only perceive a fraction
Parting invisible tissue
Viewing ourselves discretely

A plea of children is heard
Compassion and generosity
So unlike the saffron dawn
That tacitly comes and goes

We are given birth and then
Transported by our time
Existing to be just or fruitful
Vehicles of simple life

Passion romance or ideals
So much tragic demission
Flesh made of dust and shade
Our blood reddened by salt

Hundreds of days like arrows
Or universal javelins
Fly past us unobserved
Deluding our pitiful haste

We sleep for a few seconds
Lying on waterless earth
Our head resting on stone
For oblivion to restore our way

In those small hours before dawn
We expect nothing from experience
The wind suspends its voice and
Our remorse is less defined

What to tell the beloved who
Lies closely sleeping and intimate
When no kiss resolves the universe
And human effort has no effect

There are four steps we might take
To exceed this rare desperation
That of love or of seclusion
Of true kindness or deceit

Deceivers always lose themselves
Believing only in their words
The kind give away their life
Holding nothing in possession

So lovers set out at dusk
Circumventing human suffering
Stepping over sun and shade
Yet moral with anticipation

Others have weighed their hearts
Some found them wanting
Some buried their hearts
With stones taken from islands

Were we faithless in all
Our careless voluntary action
And shall our guilty expertise
Blacken the green earth at last

Palm trees and silent pines
Observe this human station
As ships vanish into the light
Sailing without any bearing

I loved you in the morning
Before you knew of me
In the noon you did not know
What lay in our embrace

Infinite and surpassing
We lightly write our names
Upon each other's body
Knowing that we cannot stay

I I I – 1 9

I STOOD there once with you
A thousand years ago
Looking out onto the plain
From that vast archway

We cover ourselves in pure cloth
Perfecting a torso received
Yet the impersonal remains
Untouched by our casual ways

Love only occurs once
Endlessly renewed by the sun
As perpetually unbound we
Pretend to be conspiratorial

Then far within the heart's core
Barely visible or conscious
The universe fits flawlessly
As we dress and undress

I knew then that time
Had graciously paused for us
Supplying those few minutes
With life imperishable

When you and I are gone
Those moments will not expire
For within that great door
Each second was entirely joined

Even when the gateway and
Its stone platform collapse
We shall remain standing there
Between so many worlds

We only act once in life
In rituals of mobility
Yet only when we love
Are we free and infinite

So what is this new sunrise
That casually holds us close
In its clear presence where
Our vision is made captive

What superhuman beauty
In its pursuit of truth
Offers us its friendship and
Reversal or conversion

As now we enter the fire
Become refined at last
Like dust thrown to the air
Is clarified of time

How is it to have no body
To be formed only of light
To always be transparent
Without adherence of pain

All the suffering we knew
All possible unhappiness
Now appears as goodness
Set against this demise

For now we wear a crown
As all the hours and minutes
Bend toward our feet
In admiration of your beauty

Evening falls onto the fields
Our mortality is not assured
One word is just required
If trust is not to betray

Life held us in its womb
Until we were free of kind
To enter upon the universe
The endless city of love

I I I – 2 0

A SOUND of rainfall pattering
At night on deck and sails
Dampness of a human soul
As it struggles toward life

A tide withdraws from us
Susurrating on the shore
Folding and unfolding with
Indigo and mercurial waves

Where reapers gather mariners
Into dry and dustless sheaves
Never to walk again across
The wet sand of their coast

So many years passed underfoot
So much vision and its sight
Ships oars harbours cities
Mysteriously beautiful islands

Unbroken rings of solitude
Infidelity of our nature
Untruth of every promise
Leading to a store of kind -

Life draws us to perfect
Our grief with simple action
Our carnal loneliness with
One just and given truth

What ingenious destination
Now draws us to its heart
Beyond human comprehension
Comfort of brief affection

Bells are always sounding
Calling us to sea and watches
Leaving only memories of
A sweet film of desire

Look   where the river turns
As the sun throws visceral gold
Then further off a scene occurs
Of love's first initiation

Like a lake in which we once
Bathed as tawny juveniles
Then slept upon the bare earth
Stripped clean by lust and appetite -

Hours and days now weave
Upon a frame of blood
As living threads issue across
A fabric of moral gravity

So rainfall surrenders
To the weight of light
As waves of human desire
Move toward an unspeakable ocean

Where mind like dawn is boundless
A shapeless flame in which
We seek the imperceptible
Crucial caress of heaven

Then in solitude and silence
There remain few distinctions
Life is singular in all direction
We believe what we dare admit -

To see the world round and visit
Those treasuries of life
Those guardians who have hidden
Their face and creep from the soul

Who guide this earth and space
With unheard gradual language
Who know how it is to unsheathe
And transform one's body

We exceed those mundane effigies
And the sea which at night is infinite
To go beyond attainment
Black beauty obverse to oblivion

There is no release now
Being so exposed and phenomenal
Not even death is possible
When our narrow airless wings -

Like huge unearthly bones
Flash and speak to us
As care and privacy trail across
The sea into the night purple

Only then with the golden skin
Which truth extinguishes
Only then does one apprehend
The mastery of life

I V - 1

THERE are three causes here
Driving us among the days
Drawing us through time
Where beauty is unspeakable

Like wind that makes us go
Are these veiled instruments –
Love of place and of person
And love without an object

The first love makes us see
Those printless signs of light
Shores hills and ground where
We might witness our return

The second love fashions us
To know what we cannot be
Our natural solitude and
Its vital pattern of affection

The final love removes us
Away from time and desire
Revealing the still universe
Apart from ourselves – reserved

These are three earthly kinds
Dimensions of the human heart
That make us mortal then
More than humanity can tell

I V - 2

THERE are two gateways here
Where we enter and depart
And our only true activity is
To give ourselves away in love

Our entrance is a living body
Beautiful with new desire
Mirror of all nature where
The unspeakable is promised

The other threshold is a song
Flashing radiant and untimed
With music and its syllables
Moving in changeless measure

It is love that makes us sing
Yet love is like the wind
Passing away among the clouds
Leaving us with its sound

Yet even the song becomes
Ineffable and we remain
Recalling its transparency
In completely mutual terms -

A beautiful vagrant harmony
Like a young hero or a hawk
Draws us off in time to where
Life shines with light sonority -

Such enduring visions of
Immutable and entire worlds
Where the still guardians of love
Surround us with their company

So all experience races past
We secure a few just moments
Allowing us to stand apart
Undeceived and never worn

Between those gateways we
Stay simply poised for a while
Between the love and the song
Which saves us from imperfection

We cross that old terrain
Going from door to door
Leaving a few bare prints
Upon the wet grass of morning

I V - 3

I THOUGHT you were the sea
As I was building my vessel
Then setting out I found
You further than horizon

Like an island you were
Or footprint on wet sand
A young bird gliding
Across the sky's truth

How long must we await
Before the ship arrives
Before our complexity
Dissolves in the sublime

The hand that made us visible
Is reaching out once more
Smoothing all cruelty
Grief at being human

For soon gone to light we are
The sun constantly ploughs
Carving furrows in all we speak
We reap little knowledge -

The intimacy and unity
Of all our moral ways
Among the pulleys of the soul
Days hold us in their arms

Unaware of what we say
Of how we walk this terrain
We are composed of breath and
The luminous within our eyes

So let us praise the men
Women who inform life
Where they walk sleep and
Disclose their affection

Let us admit to the blazing
Child who brings us signs
Warmth of an old unison
Where just years are crowned

Let us admire the swallow
Travelling through great night
Whose aim is certainly true
Bringing perfection to darkness

Let us applaud the aperture
Where time enters in a heart
That promise of humanity
Humility found in loving

Then let us commend solitude
Residence of understanding
Where the invisible sustains
All that we might ever say

As a silver ring of winter
Descends upon earth
We bend across the oars
Going out of sight

You were sea and bird
Cautious in the night
When all creatures sleep
I love to touch your face

I V - 4

SUNRISE and morning broke
And the wind across the sea
Bird-flight and light evoked
Movement from a breeze

Slowly hours simply curve
Bending with delight
As shadows walk beside us
About these invisible days

So how can we be alone
If the universe is with us
If we are never apart
From its most perfect motive

If there is no ambivalence
Even though we walk and
Speaking without words we
Present ourselves as singular

For nothing is ever lost
In all our aspiration
We simply follow time
Like birds fish or leaves

For the art of life is silent
In all our gestures and
In how we give ourselves
To what we do not know

In the night I caught a star
It cut my hands as it fell
I took the star and buried it
In the earth beneath a stone

Too light to stay this life
I weigh again our promise
Each morning in the sky
As a wind moves the air

I V - 5

WE waited for the falcon's words
In the bridal chamber of the heart
Of which no one ever speaks
And few might justly recall

So we are returned to light
And by this renewal made
To promise all demise
In the refreshment of love

Made of dust and of bone
And yet within our grain
The forces of a nameless heaven
Admit us in their way

How unbearable it is now
Not to assent to passion
To be only pursued by fiction
Like the ravening beauty of hawks

Present darkness is migrating
It is the broken season
Of clear new water rising
The arrival and return of thirst

We admit to this movement
Upon the waves of spring
Animated by the vision
Drawing sight toward the east

From winter to summer we walked
Across frozen whitened lakes
Unaware of the bird who watched
Waiting for us to close our eyes

That involuntary loss of experience
Like a shadow in the sky
Loving the wind and sunlight
And travelling clouds of rain

Into that towering fire we rise
As flames come down about us
A germ of silence in our heart
Like water touching on a shore

Time grows old and is purified
By whetstones of repeated days
That sharpen our experience
So love is not delayed

All earthly dyes suddenly
Expose their quick soft blades
The crimson and the chrome
As hard young vivid shoots

That one indestructible truth
Unspeakable here on earth
That bird of joy and victory
At the focus of the universe

I V - 6

REGARDLESS of where we go
The river is always there
Beside us as we walk - saying
I shall always love you

If only time might rotate
Backwards and we could view
All that led to our being
Our creativity here on earth

Sometimes at night the river
Turns and streams toward
Its former gentle courses
So we might renew ourselves

All the changeless experience
Of humanity and how we love
Affection that the river shares
Touching what we do not know

The river simply speaks to us
In silence with its slow ways
Like light drifting in our veins
Moving gently as it says —

I am what changes in your heart
Vision resting in your eyes
That soft mild tempo — how
It is you simply breathe

I am your small dark shadow
Pausing as the day declines
The lucid waters where you swim
As hours diminish I am night

I am the bronze leaves as they dry
The gentle green that desiccates
Slow blood that runs within - I
Am naked barefoot like the sea

I am the heron and the hawk
Always impartial in how I love
Before all worldly precedence
I am your just and inward form

Transfigured as you sleep I am
The taste of all currency
The wind as it susurrates - I
Move you with my kind

I V - 7

NOW that the light is closing
And the circumference of days
Decreases and diminishes as
Darkness moves about
And we walk the years

What grain do we leave behind
Heaped on a thin dry earth
Offering what to the future
So others might enjoy more life
Those who gave us laughter

The old voice of human suffering
Whispering for centuries
The sorrow that overcomes us
All our joy in loving and
Songs of marriage and birth

Dust and sand and emptiness
A rainless dry cold world
For night is the final condition
Of humanity and its going
Until we learn to be quite still

From lakes and channels we arrived
Beached upon this world
Beneath an arid rainfall
We drove our vessel shoreward
Pleasurably speechless

To where the sea refounds
Its source and roads are home
Going back perpetually
Truly aquiline in spirit -
Where consciousness began

We had built ourselves a ship
A boat that was unseen
So beautiful that none perceived
How it flowed and how
Perfectly it moved the sea
Attuned to a slow tempo
Of waves and full ocean

Where a bird became a fish
A girl turned to a tree
Irresistible as streams
Young men moved like water
Silent as a gliding hawk
Crossing from limb to limb

A bird rises from a stone
A fish vanishes in light
A girl strips off her leaves
To reveal perfect form
Or a young man insists
That his love is right and
Liberation a natural moment

So launch your vessel soon
We are conceived at sea
Repetition day by day
Where nothing is exclusive
Send that ship on voyages
That none can ever say
True wealth is never spoken

I V - 8

GOODNIGHT summer too long
Have you been about our walls
Swallows have departed and
Acorns shower the fields
Indestructible – your manner
Like a river between two stones
Runs away in darkness

No one moves like you
Going throughout the world
Singular and never plural
Beautiful with slow passage
Queenly in gorgeous tones
Vivid with hollow cavities -
You figure of complete life

We have walked incessantly
Your sensuous universal
Hundred-thousand years of kind
Seen the looms on which
You dress our nude skin
Our weak gentility exposed
Without your new clothing

So many boats pass by
With flags sails and oars
Flashing with your high zenith
Where now – but to be withheld
Within a broad stone cup
Upon your milky hands
As if we were libation

Where we are reaped
Our veil stripped and
Undivided we stand revealed
Made to appease your ancestors
As we are poured upon
Your lakes ponds and islands
Where children play in shallows

Horses amid brown shadowy oaks
Deer hidden beneath the wheat
A fox upon cool fine sand
Among the bitter pines
Within a curve of fern partridge
Sleep as if never wakening
Even when the sun is raving

Both seminal and fruitful
Running down-stream always
Messenger of the ideal host
Goodnight summer for now
We harvest your gaunt leaves
Your currency in this light world
All you gave us to renew

Nothing can be lost by you
Nor can it be made strict
As this life evaporates within
Your coppery cadmium rays
Tall monumental carmine clouds
From which you barely offer
To our thirst fresh rain
Coursing down across our shoulders

The rock-walls of your altar
Now shine within a rising dusk
Bats owls small quadrupeds
Commence a quiet patrol
In a sweetness of powdery air
Where stars unbind our destiny
Reminding us of absolution

For beauty once received
Cannot be retained
Is only ever ephemeral
Your vision bears just one emotion
Sorrow that such visible good
Is not acquired by devotion
Cannot ever be recalled
So goodnight dear summer

I V - 9

THE four winds about the world
That move within a human psyche
First the strange attraction going
Between male and feminine

The second takes us on in time
So that we might look back
To residence and procession
Of what was lost upon our way

The third is the emptiness
Filling up our breathing hours
And as we go toward our source
Its quietness makes us more still

The final air is that of beauty
Ephemeral quick and true
The breeze that makes substantial
Everything we cannot prove
Song of what we do not know

A hare ran under a rainbow
Swallows flew throughout the rain
Experience can be in seconds or
Even minutes and sometimes
We simply endure the years

Racing through a wet forest
Across moss and standing pools
Time or life and desire
Evade all captivity
Leaving neither scent nor trace

We cannot see our freedom
Without grey or dark it lives
Until our moral eye suddenly
Perceives the one fortune
We had assumed so long ago

A deer among cold rocks
Crossed by light and trees
The motion of a mind toward
Absent things by inclination

In true vision we cannot
Close the eyes and only
The eyebrows move showing
How wonderful is the view

I V – 1 0

TRAVELLERS can never return
To places of perfection
And those who go weeping
A cup of mere grain within
Their unbarred private heart
Endued they are one day with
Smooth fields of green wheat

Such is time's mobility
The various bones of a skull
Where three expressions tell us
Of death's weightless threshold
Its broad white gateway
Guarded by two patrolling swans

First a weakening of strength
A creaking of the vessel as
Sinew and illusion relent
Then the weariness of loving
Always surrendering our souls
Knowing we cannot be met
And finally the quiet admission
That we cannot lightly triumph
That victory too is one day closed

Ineptitude of mindless youth
Struggles of maturity and
Stillness come of slow age
And yet more durable than these
Or any stone or hard element
More firm than even old songs -

Paradise receives our bodies
The useless breath we spoke
Telling of inconsequence
Even for the unclothed lovers
Apprehensive with their bias
The beauty of joined nakedness
And those simple words

Only travellers tread paradise
For if we never move our ways
We are not transformed -
In the transit of a human soul
Is more than a world can found
More than even gravity which
Supplies our sensory wealth

The grasses and the leaves
The timber for our voyages
Children of the future
And how we tell them of our kind
Liberal fields we might describe
Where white birds stand guard
And the journey has no motive

I V – 1 1

THE mystery of sorrow and
Consciousness of private joy
We pretend there are no wounds
So we might love more fully
The rites of this living

Two souls upon a sand shore
Blue lake water at their feet
And all of light suddenly
Gracious and invisible
As it flows and covers them

The years and so much error
Small griefs not yet forgotten
Love that was never said
In profound inner silence
Luminous with passion

Life arcs overhead
Like an ardent lover causing
The world below to close
Its eyes with pauseless pleasure
The strangeness of distress saying -

'I have two souls my love and I
Who keep with me through time
Both are still and know I am
Dressed only in bare clothing
Woven of their beauty

Years are closely gathered here
Bend their necks in submission
All their lives stay and watch
As day sings and darkness weeps
Hours run away unnoticed

My soul and I meet each dawn
Vanishing so lightly
Breathless and unseeing we
Receive the beautiful
Transparence of the worldly

Where light makes no incision
This being the only kingdom
We are two souls in one
Who sustain their distinction
Such is the mystery of love's
Universal promise

Not death nor phantasy nor life
Nor absolute dismissal
Can fracture that peace now
Where we are joined by ritual
Founded on humility

I have tried by all means
To be free of the years
From words and their bodies
That captivate as lightly
As bronze midsummer grass

So I place these my breaths
In your hand like this
Loving your exception
Candid and unconcealed
Its validity unsaid

A cruciform sun arising
From saturating fog
Catches us in a circle
With yellow serum light
Revealed and justly naked

The ring a groom prepares
To be given for a bride
For no death nor any living
Can remove from this present
What was made without sorrow'

I V – 1 2

LIKE fireflies on a summer night
So our nakedness in this world
Is touched by a river lake
Sea ocean ulterior clouds
Rain streaming in threads

So too our understanding
Is circumscribed by being
Here on a stony earth
We are limited by objective
Caught by our wet blood

The void beneath a mask
Where human lust and sorrow
Are fast and consume
The naturally beautiful
Such is our poor dilemma

How solitude perplexes us
The bare extent of time
How we struggle in this moral
Silence of imperfection
For one simple diamond truth

Chromium coloured and translucent
The long blue oars of noon
As boats return and pass us
How we crave their meaning
An effulgence beyond thought

Undyed we are by daily life
Untouched by its meteors
So much procreation
Milky waves forever folding
On a tideless dry shore

The brackish taste of human love
Water of our virginity
Thorns hidden by the light
That touch us so casually
Unbreakable shell of darkness

Transfigured by affection
Or in the cry of snakes
As in our stone room sleeping
We re-enact oblivion
Each night as we embrace

There is a leopard somewhere
Who now and then reveals
Sweetness happiness and
The causeway of freedom
But then we always forget

We know it is there waiting
Observing our quiet futility
Like a slow distant thunder
On a lovely afternoon
Hinting of sudden rainfall
In the unbearable heat
So we might be remade

I V – 1 3

IN high conceptual places where
The origin and demise of life
Are caught and apprehended
The generous ones appear
As we approach and stare
At their fabulous ambition

So fame arrives on earth
With arrows and light music
Saying 'These are my prophecies
Observe now my undress'

A falcon through unbroken sky
Knowing well the full mind
Of humanity aspiring
Comes down on earth to glide
Gleaming in low morning
Catching and discharging sparks
The sun propels to this world

A perfect gazing image
Intangible and hovering there
Without tongue or limbs
It moves completely beautiful
With lucid jeweled-eyes alert

What sight can frame spaciousness
Where creatures walk and fly
Where meteors at night like grass
Swerve in transparent waves
Where the falcon stands on air

The mainstring of her waist
Releases in one gentle touch
And naked the bird is seen
All her clothing fallen down

Immaculate and desirable
She causes us to be unclothed
And we conceive in that place
Unspeakable inward joy

Like dragonflies upon a lake
Azure and emerald flight
Hawks now float upon warm air
Herons pause in aqueous shade

The wheat leans in salient fields
Cattle gather beneath trees
Tuneful with insects woods
Are bountiful and sway with life

Light is powdery alizarin
A lurid sun poised motionless
We swim out on the water
Beneath darting swallows

These soft dustless moments
When grains of incisive black
Hide within the shade
Modest now with demise

An omniscient flare of sunlight
Makes the river obsidian
Where a stringent stark aroma
Of lotos sweetens the air

Kestrels glide carelessly
Swallows think of other lands
Apples begin to thicken and
Acorns become heavy and low

'Winter begins in August'
They say as light collapses
Lengthens in the pasture and
We are inclined toward
Coolness and the closing
Of shutters and windows

Young canicular hours
Are no longer innocent
An imperative vernal love
Has accomplished its desire

Suddenly the falcon rises
Terse in the light conveying
More than this flush world
Knowing one solitary truth

Herds are waiting in the meadow
As the bird floats deliberately
Widely driven on the wind
Looking down upon our life

This manhood of the year
Womanhood of brief night
Joined by equivocation
To make each other rest

Like sparks we are crepuscular
Small flashes of compassion
Where love dashes between souls
Radiant and instantaneous

A din of dissolution
Crackles in thick darkness
Words diminish us unless
Like the falcon our aim is true

Humility patience and recession
Are the speed of this good bird
And silence the instrument
Of its elated flight

There is no going away from
The severed manners of time
Rich we are with fullness
Without guilt or one desire
Universal and so temporary

I V – 1 4

TURTLEDOVE of such radiance
Perpetual in all ways
As we observe your gentleness
Your changes all too soon are gone

In our efforts to be obvious
Like rain we appear
Descending we run away
Down paths that are too dry

There is a grove where fruit
Grows but is ungathered
Where seeds of virile goodness
Are scattered on the ground

Only in our slow devotion
Do we perceive that tree
Whilst you Turtledove remain
Careless in a green vicinity

Murmuring in low dawn
The litheness of your wings touching
In restless delicate air
As scented insects sing at night

That steep fiction of all life
Irony of our conceiving
Double truth of kind and
Our infinite evasiveness

A faithless tenancy of days
Assurance of our emptiness
Where slightly we come and go
And memories are unfounded

Like nerves or vivid wires
As years flow away like sand
Light blurs in the distance
Where birth ties its knots

So our speech is disguised
When we approach your vision
More closely less imperfectly
Certain of pre-eminence

The masks we wear at dawn
To illustrate our solitude
The manners we assume
And words we cannot say

The effects of songs cries
Or mysterious consonants
Cause us to apprehend
Your verity we barely know

What is that axiom of rite
If not a man and woman joined
Their shape locked with happiness
Where every issue is sustained

Whilst animals are pairing
Upon a weightless membrane
Like breeze the future moves
More complete than we imagine

You are for me that marriage
Absolute and combined
A rarity we cannot touch
But persistently admire

Then you reveal Turtledove
Translucent and beneficent
To me a mariner of love
Who sails far from shore

Beauty that we cannot hold
The beautiful we cannot name
Strangely out of time and
Unlike living form

Turtledove - my soul made more
Undeclared and unsigned
An agony of loving fully
That is finitely human

Too light to stay this life
As an evening gone you are
Immobile just as we become
Aware of your bounds

So graciously you withdraw
To sing before another world
Soul dripping with delight
Perfumed by the ocean's curve

Your mastery of sea and music
Measuring the full and sensuous
The giant stones along the coast
Grinding a repeating surf

Promiscuous with agitation
Just like the voice of creatures playing
Intimate but not admired
Each morning when you observe

All this I know well and keep
Within my heart for life
Even in the sun's long wake
Running into darkness

The only truth is my love
For you as sure as heaven
Deftly moving all creation
With nothing as your tide

Our speech and songs were water
That we drank and shared
Able and revived by love
Before death dried our bones

Evening came as the sun
Like a vast and ochre star
Drew up its formal pyramid
We hauled anchor once again

That ever-cleansing sea of light
Where nativity began
Vessel of our being and
All this is yours - Turtledove
Explicitly undone

I V – 1 5

ACHILLES you loved too much
You went beyond this world
Only your horses knew your way
And there was no zero at all

Transcending all daylight
You exceeded your companions
For love took you everywhere
There was no one any more

There was no possible negation
The wheels were never turning
And none of us were alone for
Your aim was always true

It was your song dear Achilles
That gave us all we needed
You excelled in experience
Beyond earthly recall

You were the only lover then
Who could walk beyond the hours
And when your horses told you
That there was no end –

Your song became beautiful
Perfectly light and sonorous
You went so far out of time
Unbound by the breath of words

Yet sometimes in the quietness
Before the sun reveals her eyes
Beyond the coast reflecting
Upon an uninhabited sea –

Forms of perfect beauty show
Themselves in grey darkness
Offering their true company
To draw you from a tense world

Like blood they are unseen
Always moving in your heart
Sublime even in your sleep
When you receive their kind

Lucid in their incidence
Without weight or anguish
Their lenience and compassion
Made you justly undesiring

So you are restored in this
Suspense of all affection
As if your body was aroused
With such transparent amity

Then when the new sun warms
All colouring of life on earth
They disappeared into the light
So your vision might return

I V – 1 6

THE king of poetry said to his bride
Be with me always just in love
So like coloured birds we live
Friends of lakes low hills and rivers

Be my lady of the rocks
Who looks down upon the plain
Where flocks and herds cross the light
As their bells echo to the sky

In that room where we sleep
Shadowed from tall zenith noon
Our bed shall be patterned with
Anemones and violets dancing

You shall wear transparent cloth
A gown through which the world appears
And in the outline of your figure
Shall beauty find a perfect measure

In the loosening of your belt
The garment from your shoulders falling
The sound of your silver bracelets
Shall keep the night from dawning

This wedding of the king and queen
Under vine leaves beside fields
Shall cause the world to see itself
And make the fame of life on earth

AFTERWORD

IN THE ART of metaphor, the act of love—whether it be of place, person, or without object—offers us our greatest scope for perception and personal expression. The work of poetry is to create such views of universal life through which we might apprehend the bare and lucid substance of our being. There, we describe something which does not exist except in a formal and harmonious state and that forceful coherence supplies us with our necessity and location, and it is this experience which makes us love. The foolishness of compulsion or domination are instrumental and delusive garments, clothing which we do not need if we might stand out of time. So why does one read or listen to poetry except to go away, to be apart from this suffering and exclusion, from the cruelty of passion and its pitiful disregard? Poetry gives us our ground and insensible terrain in this atavistic world and reminds us or reforms us with its activation of the thoroughly present and yet unspeakable but true jurisdiction which makes life and time and all our troubled love inherent and firm. Here, bitterness can be a great gift, like the wings of despair or mute anger which lift us away from ourselves. Then, at evening, as we are alone in the fields and the sun settles behind the stones and trees, as the hawks, crows, and geese pass overhead, then in our solitude we might become true. It as if we were far away at sea and the waves were not breaking and land was not in sight and we were free to love, for that is our sole act of liberty, that one untimed conception of the universe: that is, nature without instinct and unmasked.

~ GIVING IN A WORD IS FAME ~

INDEX OF FIRST LINES

Kevin McGRATH was born in southern China in 1951 and was educated in England and Scotland; he has lived and worked in France, Greece, and India. Presently he is an Associate of the Department of South Asian Studies and Poet Laureate at Lowell House, Harvard University. Publications include: *Fame* (1995); *Lioness* (1998); *The Sanskrit Hero* (2004); *Flyer* (2005); *Comedia* (2008); *Stri* (2009); *Jaya* (2011); *Supernature* (2012); *Eroica*, and *Heroic Krsna* (2013); *In the Kacch*, and *Windward* (2015); *Arjuna Pandava*, and *Eros* (2016); *Raja Yudhisthira* (2017); *Bhisma Devavrata* (2018); *Vyasa Redux* (2019); *Song Of The Republic* (2020); and *On Friendship*, and *Causality In Homeric Song* (forthcoming, 2023). McGrath lives in Cambridge, Massachusetts, with his family.

Ingram Content Group UK Ltd.
Milton Keynes UK
UKHW042239030523
421159UK00001B/11

9 781955 194129